Teaching Foundation Music

A complete, step-by-step scheme of work by Ann Bryant

International MUSIC Publications

Published 2002

Editor: Robin Norman
Music and text setting: Barnes Music Engraving Ltd.
CD: Bell Voice Recordings
Cover Design: Dominic Brookman
Illustrations: David McKee
Photography: Moose Azim

Contents

Christmas Songs and Rhymes

Appendices ....

Foreword

Although I have been a Reception teacher for over eleven years, I have always felt rather inadequate in my teaching of music, relying mainly on pre-recorded programmes or on teaching songs with the odd percussion accompaniment. I was therefore delighted when Ann asked me to trial her scheme of work for the Foundation Stage. Having worked with Ann some years ago, I had witnessed at first hand the tremendous results that she achieved musically with very young children and knew that her talent and experience would produce an excellent scheme of work. However, she is a music specialist and I am most definitely not, so it was with a certain amount of apprehension that I began.

I am pleased to say that my fears were quickly laid to rest. The introduction answered many of my questions and gave me confidence to use the correct musical terminology. The lessons are clearly set out, easy to follow, and allow for flexibility if time is short. But the most important aspect for me has been to witness the absolute delight and enjoyment experienced by my class as we have progressed through the scheme week by week. The initial excitement has remained, but as a routine has been established, the children approach each lesson in a calm and responsible way. It has been very rewarding for me to see the children participating with such enthusiasm, and many of the songs have become firm favourites, being sung in the playground and classroom alike! The children even asked to perform *Boogie Bugs* to the rest of the school in a showing assembly, and the song was an instant hit with both children and adults.

I am sure that anyone working with children in the Foundation Stage, whatever their musical background, will find that this scheme of work will enrich their teaching, and I encourage you all to read on...

Mandy Norgrove
East Farleigh Primary School

As a non-musician I find the book easy to follow as each session is adaptable to meet the needs of the differing age groups. It is not difficult, either, to work the book around themes or current events. This is the first time I have felt confident teaching music in nursery, and I am finding the children very responsive, often asking me to repeat a previous sessions which they particularly enjoyed. In my opinion this book will be invaluable to both musical and non-musical staff who work with pre-school/nursery children. It is certainly the best resource I have used for a long time - or even ever!

Sarah Warner
Pre-school Nursery Manager
Great Pagehurst Pre-School Nursery

Acknowledgements

Thank you very much, Pat Hutchins, for allowing me to base my song 'The Great Big Woods' on your book 'Goodnight, Owl!'

My grateful thanks to Mandy Norgrove (Reception), Sarah Warner (Nursery) and Carol Grey (Nursery and Reception) for all their help in the preparation of this book.

Thanks too, to Jonathan Cohen, Steve Hall, Diana Gabriel, Holly and Hannah Pilkington, Lucy and Amy Baxter, and my daughter, Jody, who all feature on the CD and who helped make the recording sessions such a pleasure. Special recognition to my colleagues Karen Puzey and Jacqui Marriott. I couldn't do what I do half as effectively without you, thank you both.

Ann Bryant

Introduction

If I'm not a specialist, how can I teach music?

You don't have to know anything about music to deliver a rich and varied course of music to the Foundation Stage age group. What you *do* need is confidence and guidance, and that is what this book aims to give you. It will take you step by step through a progressive course that will allow you to take charge of your music teaching, to separate out the various strands of skills being covered in any activity, and to evaluate progress. All the songs included in the scheme are on the CD, so there is no need to read music.

I have talked with many teachers, supervisors and helpers working with the Foundation Stage age group and am often told, 'We don't really do music, but we do singing.' On further questioning I find that a random selection of finger rhymes and action songs and the like are being taught, but the teacher/supervisor is unsure as to whether the work they are doing is valuable, and if so, why. Many teachers also feel insecure about assessing whether progress is being made.

Some leaders question, quite rightly, the value of sound tables, where children can go along at free will, pick up an instrument and explore its sound. Realistically, there is never a high enough teacher/pupil ratio to make this workable, and it can even become counter productive if this 'exploration' is abused and the sounds become nothing more than an intrusive and irritating background noise, which serves to dull the senses of the children. The kind of exploration of sound carried out in this context is more suitable for 0–2 year olds.

Music through play

It is now widely accepted that children learn through play, so you will find a great many games in this book. You might have thought Musical Bumps was a frivolous party activity (!) but think of the skills involved:

1. Recognising that music is being played. (Not as obvious as it seems. Music is a constant background in many homes, and the child's aural sense can become dulled)
2. Realising that the start of the music is the signal to move around the room dancing or skipping
3. Noticing that the music has stopped, and sitting down
4. Learning to anticipate the music stopping, while maintaining movement
5. Moving to reflect the style/beat of the music
6. Increasing reaction speed in order to sit down as quickly as possible
7. Understanding that to sit down quickly is to avoid elimination, and so stand a chance of winning the game!

You will see from the above that musical skills and life skills overlap considerably, because music has so much to do with awareness, alertness, listening and co-ordination. There is also a great deal of evidence to suggest that co-ordination skills are valuable in helping overcome dyslexia.

Listening skills

The skill of listening is arguably the most important life skill, and music is the best subject through which to develop this skill. I believe that *all* children are born with some degree of musicality. When I first start to teach music to a new intake of three- or four-year-olds, I see a very wide ability range. By the time these children have completed Year 1, a kind of levelling has happened, in that *all* the children have mastered basic listening skills and are used to listening instinctively.

The value of singing

Songs and rhymes are the best musical 'tools' for very young children. We sing because it is such an enjoyable thing to do, but also because it is a release for emotions. Through singing children gradually gain self-confidence, and develop their sense of rhythm and pitch as well as improving their literacy skills.

The National Curriculum (Foundation Stage) makes strong connections between music and art and craft/ movement but fails do so between music and literature/language. And yet songs are a fusing together of rhythmic, rhyming words with music.

How to use this book

People working with children at Foundation Stage find themselves in a variety of circumstances – playgroups, nurseries and schools, teaching only one year group, teaching more than one year group, teaching different children for different lengths of time each week etc. I have designed the book to be as flexible as possible to work in these various situations. One music session takes up either a single or a double page. Each session comprises a 20-minute section, followed by an optional 10 minutes of extension work. There are a total of 60 sessions. 10 sessions equate to approximately one term.

Because the scheme is progressive I recommend starting at the beginning whenever you first come across the book, (even if you are only teaching Reception aged children), and working through session by session. However, according to your situation and your circumstances that particular day, you may choose to do only the basic part of each session or to add some or all of the extension work. It doesn't matter if you don't complete a session all in one go, and of course, it is always valuable to repeat all or part of a session for reinforcement, and to keep coming back to popular songs/activities. Particularly in a playgroup situation, you might decide to simply repeat a whole session later in the week. This consolidation work is a form of extension in itself.

Organising your music session

The music session must be a time for bringing the children together and working with them in one big group. If you have a small hall, that is perfect. If you do not have use of a hall, create as much space as possible by moving furniture. If your school hall happens to be large, try to create a 'boundary' so you are working in a more confined area. It is important to keep all the children 'with you' during the session.

It is also important to cut out all background noises. Every helper must be involved, rather than using the time to set up the next session, which will inevitably create noise, however small. The first aim is to cultivate respect for sound. This can only work on a background of silence. The sessions must have a magical feeling of everyone being involved together. So, for example, when you give out the instruments for a percussion activity, if even one child in the circle is 'twiddling' their instrument, it will spoil the atmosphere you are seeking to create.

To make music, to enjoy music and to develop musical skills, the ear must be trained, and sensitivity and awareness must be turned full on. The younger the child when this process is begun, the greater their potential will always be.

When a session is particularly movement/action based, (such as the very first session) if at all possible the children should have bare feet to keep the noise level to a minimum. If this is not practical, encourage the children to keep still between activities. As well as reducing the noise level, this will breed better listening and a greater sensitivity within the group.

The songs

Most of the sessions comprise a song or a rhyme, which generally forms the 'meat' of that session. The order of the songs is progressive. It is not, however, always the case that the songs become progressively more difficult: it is the *treatment* of the songs, which dictates the progression.

The songs cover a wide range of topics/themes, so that if at any time you want a song to go with a particular topic, and it appears much later in the book, then by all means use it. So in this respect the book is designed to function as a general resource book as well as a music course. A few Christmas songs/rhymes appear at the back. I have deliberately avoided including them in the body of the scheme, because it might not necessarily be Christmas time when you arrive at those songs in the book!

Using the CD

Children of this generation risk growing up knowing a great many words to a small number of tunes, because nowadays there are many songs around which use traditional tunes and nursery rhymes with original lyrics. The CD accompanying this book has allowed me to include plenty of original tunes, and just a handful of traditional ones.

I would advise you to listen to any new songs on the CD, as they come up, before the session. You might then want to let the children sing along with the CD, or you might prefer to teach them the song yourself and sing unaccompanied. It's up to you. The CD version might be sung either too quickly or too slowly for your particular group of children, in which case it would definitely be advisable to sing unaccompanied when you are sure of how the song goes. With some songs there is no 'built-in' ending, and it is up to you how many repetitions of the song you do. In these cases the CD plays the song once or twice through, then fades.

Tips when teaching singing

Generally speaking, the younger the child, the slower you will need to sing, though children do love trying sometimes to sing fast. They might not be able to keep up, but they will still enjoy the experience of hearing a lively, pacy song. It is worth remembering that even when a child is not physically singing they are 'involved' in the song.

Don't start a song too low yourself. I have often heard *Happy Birthday to You* sung enthusiastically by the few adults in the room, who are entirely oblivious that the children joining in are half singing and half speaking an approximation of the tune because the key is too low for them. As you gain in confidence, try starting on a higher note. Be aware of this and see what's right for your children. On your own at home sing *Happy Birthday to You* starting in 3 different places in your voice – we say that you are singing in a different key or at a different pitch.

Equally, small children's voices often don't have many high notes. Listen out for those children who *can* sing higher notes in tune, as this is a strong indicator of musicianship.

Planning

Long-term objectives

The main aim of teaching music to young children is for all the children to enjoy music (as listeners, creators and performers), be discerning listeners and most importantly of all, to feel the thrill of their newly acquired musical skills.

By the end of the Foundation Stage children should:

1. Be in the habit of listening, anticipating, concentrating, looking, and focusing
2. Be able to work within a rhythmic framework, keeping in time with a simple beat, and changing easily to a faster or slower beat
3. Be familiar with the sounds of a number of percussion instruments and be able to play the instruments, making a sound that is appropriate within the context of the music at the time
4. Have respect for the sounds they are producing, and have the self-discipline not to play their instrument until their sound is required
5. Be able to sing with an ever-developing sense of pitch
6. Be developing their skills of co-ordination.
7. Be developing quicker musical responses in general
8. Be developing in confidence.

Medium-term objectives

These will always reflect the long term aims, so to avoid unnecessary repetition, these appear as the **Focus** at the start of each batch of ten sessions.

Short-term objectives

At the beginning of each session you will see the headings **Concept**, **Theme** and **Resource**. In each case the theme will be reflected in the song/rhyme of the session.

What else will I find in the book?

At the back of the book you will find:

1. Music pages
2. Christmas songs and rhymes
3. A list of themes
4. A list of the songs/rhymes and in which session they appear
5. CD track listing.

A few musical terms explained simply

1. What is PULSE?

Start clapping now… Make sure your claps are evenly spaced. You have created a pulse. Clap more slowly, but still with regular time spaces between each clap. Now you are clapping to a slower pulse.

2. What is a BEAT?

Each one of those evenly spaced claps you've just done is a beat. You can also say, 'Keep to the beat', which is another way of saying, 'Keep to the pulse' (just to confuse you).

3. What is TEMPO?

Tempo is the speed at which you are playing or singing. You can play or sing at a slower or faster tempo.

4. What is METRE?

Choose any speed and start clapping evenly again. Now keep clapping at the same speed, but count 1, 2, 3 repeatedly as you clap and make all the number 1s louder than the 2s and 3s. Now you have a metre. You are clapping in 3-time. Change your counting to go up to 4 each time, and make sure the 1s are louder than the 2s, 3s and 4s. Now you are clapping in 4-time. This is the most commonly-used metre and so is often called Common time. You will have often heard the expression 'Keep in time'. It means keep on the beat or keep a steady pulse as you play or sing. Remember that the children won't know what you mean when you first use this expression!

5. What is RHYTHM?

Clap *Happy Birthday to You*. You are doing more than just clapping a pulse or even a metre. You are arranging claps of different speeds into a pattern. This pattern is a rhythm. In another sense you can also say 'She's got good rhythm' which means she clearly feels the pulse, the beat, the metre, the general flow of the music, and is interpreting it accurately.

6. What is PITCH?

Sing *Happy Birthday to You*. You are singing higher and lower notes – i.e. notes of different pitch. This particular pattern of pitched notes combined with the rhythmic pattern is the composition for the song *Happy Birthday to You*.

7. What is TIMBRE?

Timbre simply means the quality of a musical sound. Claves have a wooden, clacking timbre, drums a thuddy, deeper timbre and bells a high, tinkling timbre etc.

8. What are DYNAMICS?

Dynamics is the musical term for how loudly or quietly you sing or play.

9. What is OSTINATO?

A repeated rhythmic idea used to accompany a piece of music.

Using percussion instruments

You will need a xylophone or a glockenspiel for yourself, and enough instruments for every child in your group to have one each. In the course, the percussion instruments are sometimes used to play on the beat and sometimes to provide sound 'colour'. For the purposes of the latter, the more sounds you have the better, including homemade instruments. There are some wonderful instruments, specifically designed with small hands in mind, available to buy nowadays.

For keeping to a beat it is best to have simple instruments that produce one clear sound at a time. I would recommend:

- **6 small tambourines**
- **6 tambours/hand drums with beaters:** These are the little drums which look like tambourines but without bells.
- **6 maracas or shakers:** These could be made from empty yoghurt pots, or a similar container, filled, a

centimetre at the most, deep with dry rice or dry pasta. The type, the size and the contents of the container will dictate the different sounds they make. Making shakers and decorating them is a great activity in itself, especially if you try to make two which sound exactly the same. Having said that, there are some wonderful little shakers on the market nowadays.

- **12 wooden instruments:** Either claves, which are just two cylindrical sticks which can be tapped together or a simple wood block, which is a block of wood tapped with a wooden beater. You can create a similar sounding wooden instrument with something as simple as two wooden spoons or spatulas tapped against each other.

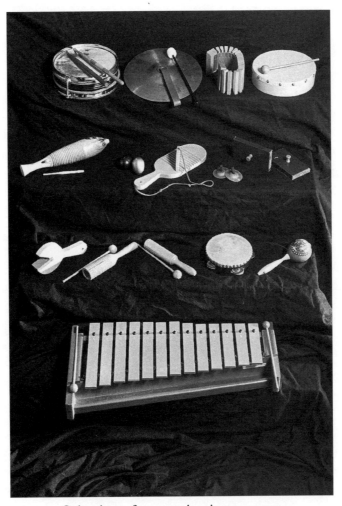

Selection of percussion instruments

Tips when playing instruments

I am deliberately not going into great detail here about the correct way to hold instruments, because for small children, the most manageable way is the correct way. I would just say, do explore the various sounds produced when you handle instruments in different ways, and make sure that this is a consideration.

A **tambourine** played with a flat hand, for example, makes a different sound from when it is played with fingertips. Personally I prefer the latter. A **tambour/hand drum** makes a different sound when beaten on the floor from when held in the hand and beaten. Small children find **large cymbals** difficult to handle. I would recommend playing one large one with a beater, rather than two clashed together. Take care to hold the cymbal so no part of it touches the child's body, or that will stop it from ringing on. With little **finger cymbals**, if you play them like two mini cymbals, it is important not to keep them together but to pull them apart the moment they have clanged against each other, so that the sound can ring on. If you play them with an up and down action, they will make a purer sound. For rhythmic work I find small **shakers/maracas** with a handle the best, so that the child can tap the shaker into the palm of the other hand. This makes a cleaner sound. Shaking it with one hand only tends to make two sounds at a time. Later in the book I introduce **chime bars/glocks** in a very limited way. When playing these, take care to bounce the beater, rather than letting it rest on the bar, and try to aim for the centre of the bar and don't hit it with too much force.

Chapter 1
Sessions 1–10

Focus:
- Tuning in!
- Reacting quickly
- Quiet/Loud
- Introducing percussion instruments
- Recognising and matching a beat
- The rhythm of words

Songs/rhymes: *Cool Cats; Crackers; Musical Parade; Working Away; How Many Toys?; We're Going on a Holiday; Counting Up the Birthdays; The Birthday Song; The Shape Song; The Wind*

Session 1

Concept:
- Look and listen
- Quiet/Loud

Theme: Cats; Crackers

Resource: A drum and also a toy cat or picture of a cat

Being very, very quiet!
- This first session will set the tone for all your music sessions. Try to establish right from the start a sense of the magic of working all together, creating sounds on a background of silence. The children should sit in a group. Wait till they are completely quiet. Talk in a quiet voice. Show a picture of a cat or hold up a toy cat and explain how cats move so quietly that if you had your eyes closed you wouldn't hear a sound. Ask the children to see how quietly they can do the things you say. Give instructions to stand up, find a space, and creep. Stop after each of these, to observe and praise their efforts. Try to keep your voice at a whisper in the process! Pick out anyone doing it particularly silently to demonstrate.
- Now tell the children you are going to tap your drum (hand drum) very quietly indeed and they must creep on tiptoe round the room, but they mustn't start till you start and they must stop the very second you stop.
- Try that once or twice, encouraging them to keep listening as they creep, so they'll stop at exactly the right moment.

Cool Cats

Cats arch their backs up and down	*on all fours, arch backs*
Cats like to stretch their claws	*kneel (bottoms on feet) and 'stretch claws'*
Cats creep softly, gently, gingerly	*crawl very slowly and smoothly*
Cats lick their velvet paws	*stop, kneel, pretend to lick paws*
Cool cats, smooth and smart	*stand up as smoothly as possible and stretch arms up*
Let's go, back to the start	*kneel back down again as smoothly as possible*

- Say the above poem, while doing the actions yourself, and encourage the children to join in. You will feel the natural rhythm of the words. The first two words of the last two lines need to be spoken slowly to maintain the rhythm.

Crackers

Pull the cracker one, two, three!
Tom★ jumps out and shouts 'It's me!'

- Sit in a circle. Say the *Crackers* rhyme and do the actions below:

ALL: Pull the cracker, one, two, three!	*Do quiet claps on 'one, two'*
	then a sudden loud one as everyone shouts 'three!'
TEACHER: Chloe (★a different name each time) jumps out and shouts…	
CHLOE: (*jumping up*) It's me!	

- Repeat several times with different children jumping up and calling, 'It's me!' Ask the children what was the difference between the *Cats* activity and the *Crackers* activity. (One was quiet and one loud.)

Extension

Pass the drum around
- First, show the children how to tap the right number of taps on the drum to match their first name. Demonstrate how your name sounds, e.g. MISS-IS BROWN (3 taps).
- Now play music of your choice and pass a drum round the circle. When the music stops the child holding the drum should say their name while tapping the right number of taps on the drum to match e.g. EM-I-LY would be 3 taps, JACK would be 1. It doesn't matter about getting the right number of taps at this stage, though it is a valuable added focus. The main aim here is to make an individual contribution. Continue like this.

Finish with a well known song
- Sing any song you know, deciding beforehand if it will be sung quietly or loudly.

Session 2

Concept:
- Quiet/Loud
- Introducing percussion instruments

Theme: Copycats

Resource: A wide range of percussion instruments (2–4 of each type, enough for one each)

Introducing the instruments

- Prepare by sitting in a circle and putting the instruments in the middle. With a group of 20 children you might, for example, have:

2 tambourines
3 drums
3 pairs of finger cymbals
3 shakers
4 wood blocks
3 claves
2 cymbals

- It is vital that the children understand the importance of sound and silence and that they learn to respect the instruments right from the word go. Explain that the instruments are precious and need careful handling, and also that any sound coming from a musical instrument should be thought about and listened to. Fiddling with the instrument is strictly not allowed! The following rhyme is useful when emphasising this rule:

> If you play before I say,
>
> You will find I take it away!

Ask the children to chant this important little poem with you. Every time you use the instruments, say the poem, and if anyone breaks the rule, take their instrument away for a minute or two. (I have always found that being ruthless in these early stages encourages good habits!)

Playing by copying

- Take one of every type of instrument and place the others, one in front of each child, at random. Choose one of the instruments to play. The children must watch you carefully to see which instrument you are playing. They should only join in if they have the same instrument in front of them. They should copy exactly what you play. Tell them that even when they've had one go, they might still get another later on. This keeps them concentrating.
- Where possible play each instrument in more than one way. For example play a tambourine first by shaking it, then by tapping it; shakers can be shaken continuously or intermittently; some wooden instruments can be scraped or tapped. Sometimes play loudly, sometimes quietly. Try playing steady, even beats for the children to copy, but don't worry if they are not able to match your beat. The important factors here are having the confidence to play, and the discipline to play at the right times. Keep checking no-one is twiddling his or her instrument. Try being completely silent and still and see who can hear the clock ticking or other subtle sounds.

Quick reactions

- Play quiet taps on the drum. The children should tiptoe around to the sounds of the drum. Join in with them so they can follow your example and 'match' their steps to the beat of the drum. They should be listening for when you stop playing, which means they should also stop, or if you play a sudden loud tap, which means they should make an interesting shape as quickly as possible. Discourage jumping into a shape, so the shape can be made as quickly as possible.

Extension

- Put your instruments in a sack so the children can't see which one you are playing. Repeat the above activity but see if the children know whose turn it is to play by listening only!
- Try the rhyme *Crackers* but instead of doing the two quiet claps and then one loud one, make two quiet sounds on your instruments, followed by one loud one.

Who's turn to play?

15

Session 3

Concept:
- Getting used to percussion instruments
- Loud

Theme: A musical parade!

Resource: Enough instruments for one each. CD track 1

Musical Parade
Tune: This Old Man

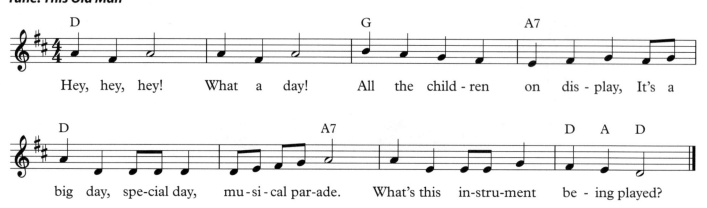

- The children should sit in a circle with an instrument in front of each of them. Remind them about the no twiddling rule.
- Sing the song all together. At the end, call out the name of an instrument e.g. tambourines. Those children with tambourines should then play their instruments while the others all clap along to the music. CD track 1 gives opportunity for five 'sing-throughs'. I call out 'tambourines' at the end of the first run-through. This is the cue for the tambourines to play the beat while everybody sings the song through again. At the end of the subsequent sing-throughs, I leave it to you to call out the name of a different instrument e.g. claves. The claves would then play the beat for the next sing-through, and so on. So if you are using the CD, make sure you only have four different types of instrument, in order to allow every child to get the chance to play. In this and subsequent sessions use of the CD is entirely optional. You might want to use it at first and then sing without it.

Throughout these first sessions, encourage the children to play 'in time' to the music rather than just bashing the instrument! Keep asking if they are listening to the music and trying to make their playing fit in well. At this stage, though, it is better to sacrifice precision of beat, if necessary, to focus on enjoyment and joining in at the right time.

Extension

- Try the song in a slightly different way. This time, ask the children playing instruments to march round the circle at the same time.
- Repeat the 'Pass the drum around' activity from Session 1.
- This time when the music stops the child holding the drum should look at you. If you have a finger to your lips, they should say their name in a quiet voice (just loud enough for everyone to hear) while quietly tapping the right number of taps on the drum to match their name e.g. EM-I-LY would be 3 taps, JACK would be 1. If you cup your hands around your mouth (as though showing a loud hailer), the children should say their name loudly, matching it with loud drum taps. Again it doesn't matter about getting the right number of taps at this stage. The main aim here is to make an individual Quiet/Loud contribution. Continue like this.

Session 4

Concept:
- Co-ordinating actions and sung words

Theme: Household jobs

Resource: One instrument for each child (ideally half shakers and half wooden sounding instruments); CD track 2

Working Away

1. Sweep-ing, sweep-ing, sweep-ing a-way, sweep-ing a-way, sweep-ing a-way.

Sweep-ing, sweep-ing, sweep-ing a-way, till the work's all done and we can play.

2. Scrubbing, scrubbing . . .
3. Wiping, wiping . . .
4. Baking, baking . . .
5. Ironing, ironing . . .

Singing *Working Away* with actions

- The children should stand in a space of their own. Call out what the activity is going to be each time, then sing through with the relevant actions. Try to make the action a repeated one that fits the beat of the music. On the words 'work's all done' ask the children to fold their arms. On the word 'we' they should tap their chests with both hands then on the word 'play' stretch both hands out in front.

'Baking away'

Accompanying *Working Away* with instruments

- Ask the children to sit in a circle, each with an instrument in front of them. Ideally half the children should have a wooden sounding instrument of one sort or another, and the other half should have some sort of shaker. If this is not possible it doesn't matter. Half the children should play their instruments, trying to keep in time with the beat of the music, while the other half sing verse 1. Then swap for verse 2. Swap back for verse 3 and so on.

It is a good idea to sit in a circle and talk about an activity/song when you have done it once. Simple questions such as 'Was anyone playing too loudly/quietly?' and 'Did it sound nice?' encourages the beginning of musical awareness and critical evaluation.

Extension

- Divide the children into three groups, but only give instruments to the first group.
- Everyone should sing verse 1 while the first group tap the beat on the instruments. During verse 2 the three groups swap round one place, leaving the instruments put. For this 'swapping round', encourage the children to tiptoe. While everybody then sings verse 3, the second group should play the instruments, then swap places again during verse 4, and finally the third group should play during verse 5.

Session 5

Concept:

- Quick reactions

Theme: Counting up and down

Resource: Five small toys; CD track 3; xylophone/glockenspiel; shaker

How Many Toys?
Tune: Skip To My Lou

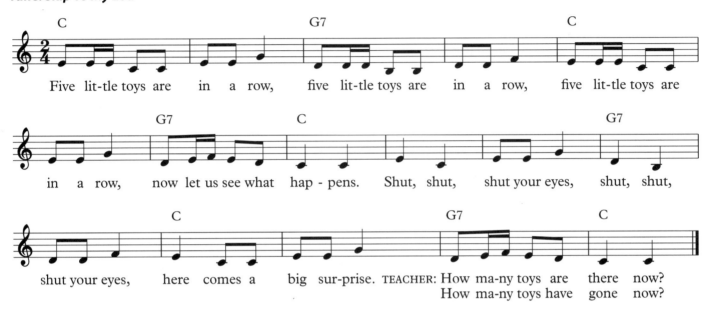

- Line up five toys in a row so that the children can see them, then sing the song together. When you sing 'Shut your eyes' encourage the children to shut their eyes so you can add or take away one or more toy, according to the children's counting level. At the end of the line 'Here comes a big surprise' the children should open their eyes and shout out how many toys they can see. Repeat the verse singing the new number of toys. On the CD the song is played through four times. The lack of vocal line in the second, third and fourth play-throughs allow you to add or take away toys as you want.
- Later in the course, as the children become more confident, you might want to challenge them to say how many toys are *missing*, and use a greater number than five as a starting point.

Children with eyes shut while I move fifth toy away

19

Which instrument will it be?

- Sit in a circle and give each child an instrument. You will need four different types. Children holding the same type of instrument should sit next to each other. Sing verse 1 with the CD. At the end, when the children have called out how many toys are there, *you* call out the name of an instrument. The children must be alert to hear whether you choose their instrument. They should be looking at you and holding their instruments ready to play. Those children with instruments of the name you call should play the beat during verse 2. And so on.

Signals

- Play the highest note (smallest bar) on the xylophone or glockenspiel and ask the children to touch their heads. Now play the lowest note and ask the children to touch their toes. Now play a shaker with a stirring action and ask the children to turn round once. Explain the connection between the sound and the action in each case.
- Now try this activity. The children should stand in their own space and get ready to listen. When they hear you play one of the sounds, they must try to remember which action goes with that sound and do the action as fast as possible.

Extension

- Add one or two more signals on different instruments and make the activity into an elimination game. The slower children and/or those who got it wrong are 'out'. See who is the winner at the end.

Session 6

Concept:
- Verse/chorus

Theme: Holidays

Resource: CD track 4. From now on, always have the percussion instruments at the ready. They will not specifically be mentioned under 'resource'

We're Going on a Holiday
Tune: I Saw Three Ships

1. We're staying in a caravan . . .
   We're setting off in the morning.
   CHORUS

2. We're staying in a big hotel . . .
   CHORUS

3. We're staying on a camping site . . .
   CHORUS

4. We're staying in a seaside house . . .

- Sing the song through. You might like to skip slowly round while singing the chorus each time, then stand still in different parts of the room, as though on holiday in the various locations.
- Sit down in a circle with the instruments in the middle. Explain in simple terms, the concept of verse and chorus. The repeated section about 'going on a holiday' is the chorus. The sections between, which have different words each time are called the verses. How many different holiday locations can the children remember?

Playing instruments with the song
- Divide the class into four groups. Each group should have a different set of instruments if possible. Sing the song through again and this time, the groups take turns to accompany the verses, (adult voices on the CD) and *all* the children should play during the chorus each time, (children's voices on the CD). The beat is quite slow. Encourage careful listening to accompany with a steady, even beat in time with the music, but again, at this stage the joining in at the right moment and the enjoyment factor are the chief objectives.

Extension

- Put the instruments back into the middle of the circle and try this activity. Choose a child to skip round the outside of the circle while everyone else sings and claps (to the same beat) during the chorus. When the chorus ends, that child sits down in the circle at whichever place he/she has arrived at, and touches the child next to him. Now this child must get up and skip round the circle until the end of verse 1. Continue like this. At first the children might be slow to get up and get going when it is their turn, so they won't get very far round the circle! With practice these reactions will speed up.

Session 7

Concept:
- Being ready to play at exactly the right moment
- Making up words to fit a tune

Theme: Birthdays; Counting up

Resource: CD tracks 5 and 6; five dolls and/or cuddly toys

Counting Up the Birthdays

El - lie Jane is one to - day, one to - day, one to - day.

El - lie Jane is one to - day, it's her birth - day.

Make up your own verses depending on your toys/dolls.
e.g. Big brown bear is two today . . .
it's his birthday.

- In the song, *Counting Up the Birthdays,* we have named the doll/toy in the first verse 'Ellie Jane'. When you've selected five toys/dolls, sit down with the children and decide which one should be called Ellie Jane. Then name the other four, making sure that each name has three syllables so it fits into the rhythm of the melody e.g. HAIR-Y DOG or BIG BROWN BEAR. Ellie Jane is one, as we know from the lyrics (!) Now decide which character is two years old, and so on up to five. Line the toys/dolls up accordingly.
- Sing the song straight through incorporating into the lyrics the names of your toys/dolls and their ages, as demonstrated in verse 1 on the CD. There are five play-throughs of the song but only verse 1 is actually sung, so as not to interfere with your chosen words.

Which instrument will it be?
- Sit in a circle and give each child an instrument. You will need four different types. Do the activity 'Which instrument will it be?' from Session 5, where you call out the name of a type of instrument at the end of each verse and those children with that type of instrument should then play the beat during the following verse.
- Now ask the children to pick up their instruments and swap places in the circle. Sing the song again. A little more individual responsibility is needed from the children, to be aware of when to play, as they are isolated from the rest of those children with the same instrument.

Actions – 8 lots of 8
- In music, the skill of coming in at the right moment within a rhythmic framework is a fundamental one. Try this activity to develop that skill: The children should sit in a space of their own and listen to track 6 of the CD. They will instinctively come to feel the musical sections (or phrases, to use the correct term). There are 8 sections, each one 8 beats long. Ask the children to copy the actions you do. Choose a different action for each phrase and do that action 8 times to fit the duration of the phrase. You might do 8 claps, 8 marches on the spot, 8 knee taps etc.
- As you repeat this activity you might be able to decide on the actions beforehand and see if you can all change at the same moment to the next one. This is a good memory tester as well.

Extension

Playing instruments with *Counting Up the Birthdays*

- Try introducing more different types of instrument into the song, so the individual responsibility becomes greater still. If you want, you can dispense with the name of the instrument altogether and simply say a child's name at the end of each verse.

A variation on the 'Actions' activity

- Suggest to the children that they do the activities, in whichever order they like as long as they change to a different one when they hear the new phrase starting each time.
- Can the children think of any more actions?

Session 8

Concept:
- Co-ordination
- Being ready to respond at exactly the right moment
- The rhythm of words

Theme: The month you are born in
Resource: CD track 7

The Birthday Song

Go - ing to   a par - ty,   sit - ting in   a cir - cle,   who's it going to be,   let's   see.

TEACHER: If you've got   a birth-day   in the month of *Aug-ust,   stand up and shout: 'That's me!'

SHOUT: That's me!

* teacher calls out a different month each time

- First sit down in a circle and talk about birthdays. The idea is for all the children to recognise the sound of the month in which their birthday lies! This is a tall order and you might like to group the children accordingly at first, then sit them randomly when they recognise their birth month. On the CD the song is played through just once as a demonstration, choosing the month of August.
- Sing the song repeatedly, working on the skill of jumping up quickly at the end each time, and calling out 'That's me!' in time with the established beat.
- While singing the song, try to co-ordinate the following repeated actions – 1 tap on knees followed by 1 clap. Some children will find this difficult and might prefer to concentrate on the actions without having to sing, or vice versa. Make sure you are consistent about starting with the tap, rather than the clap.

'That's me'

The rhythmic sounds of two contrasting months

- Take two different sounding months such as January and May. Play each one on a hand drum while saying it, to emphasise the difference. Ask the January children to sit in one group and the May children in another. Play one of those two months on the drum. Can the right child/group of children jump up if you play theirs? Ask those children watching to say whether the right children responded.
- Now try with two months which sound less obviously different such as February and December.

Extension

- All sit down together and clap and chant rhythmically:

  JAN-U-A-RY JAN-U-A-RY MAY MAY

  JAN-U-A-RY JAN-U-A-RY MAY MAY etc.

- Now sit in a circle, each child with a random instrument. All play the rhythm you have just clapped on the instruments. Try playing the rhythm a few times quietly then a few times loudly. Ask the children to watch you carefully. If your palms face downwards they should play quietly. If you raise your hands with your palms facing upwards they should play loudly.

It is difficult for small children to play instruments quickly so choose a slow speed for this exercise. Always make the actions of tapping or scraping or whatever very small when you want to play quickly.

Session 9

Concept:
- The rhythm of words
- Co-ordination

Theme: Shapes

Resource: CD track 8

The Shape Song
Tune: Poor Jenny Sits a-weeping

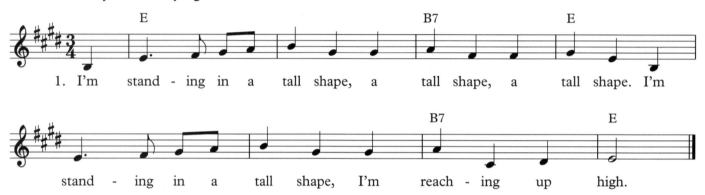

1. I'm stand-ing in a tall shape, a tall shape, a tall shape. I'm stand-ing in a tall shape, I'm reach-ing up high.

2. I'm standing in a wide space . . .
   I'm stretching out wide.

3. I'm sitting in a small shape . . .
   I'm curling up small.

4. We're standing in a circle . . .
   We're all holding hands.

5. We're crouching in a frog shape . . .
   We're ready to jump.

6. We're sitting in a circle . . .
   Going pat, clap, clap, pat!

- The children should start in a space of their own and make the individual shapes that the words suggest as they sing. When it comes to verse 4, make the class circle calmly and slowly. For verse 6, 'going pat clap clap pat', pat your knees then do 2 claps and finish by patting your knees again. This is difficult to co-ordinate (see extension activity).

Animals with different sounding names

- Verse 5 of this song mentions frogs. Sit down in a circle and talk about animals which have a different number of sounds/syllables in their names. Frog has 1 sound, monkey has 2, crocodile has 3. By tapping a drum and counting, make sure the children understand this. Now play a game where the children must listen for how many taps you do, and represent that animal by making an appropriate shape. Crouch like a frog, hands on the floor between legs. The crocodile could be shown by both arms out straight in front, one high, one low, representing the crocodile's jaws. Picture a monkey hanging by its tail and bend forwards from the waist with one arm high representing the tail.

Extension

Co-ordinating actions and singing

- Sit in a circle. Practise doing 1 pat on the knees, followed by 2 claps and repeating that sequence over and over, very slowly at first. See if everyone can keep together and keep an even beat. Now, try maintaining these actions in time to the song on the CD (track 8). This is very tricky and will be reinforced later in the course.

Session 10

Concept:
- Quiet and Loud
- Using percussion to convey sound 'colour' as opposed to keeping with a beat

Theme: Windy weather

Resource: Instruments to include 1–3 xylophones or glockenspiels; CD track 9

The Wind

Raindrops falling, raindrops falling,
Wind is stirring, wind is stirring,
Leaves are rustling, leaves are rustling,
Shutters banging, shutters banging.
Branches creaking, branches creaking,
Rain and leaves are swirling, whirling
Wind is really causing havoc…
Wind has gone and all is calm.

Putting actions with the poem
- Standing in spaces, try the poem with the following actions:

Line:
1. Shaking fingers (descending action)
2. Sway gently while rolling hands over and over very slowly
3. Bend low and shake fingers close to the ground
4. Straighten up and clap hands from straight wide armed position
5. Make shape of gnarled old tree!
6. Going high and low and turning round on the spot with shaking fingers
7. As 6, but moving round room
8. Stop and gently, slowly, kneel and curl right over. Stay still for a few seconds.

'Branches creaking'

27

Using percussion to convey sound colour

- Sit in a circle with the instruments in the centre. Explain that we are going to be using the sounds of the instruments in a different way this time. Instead of making a beat to accompany a song, we are making sounds to bring the words of the poem alive.

- Say each line of the poem and discuss with the children which instruments would best convey the words of that line. Remember it is the sound quality (or timbre, to use the musical word!) of the instrument, as well as the way the instrument is played (in this case focusing on loudly or quietly) which are the important factors in the choice of instruments.

- Now say the poem very slowly, accompanied by groups of children playing the chosen instruments. There is an illustration below but feel free to make your own choice of instruments! The children will find it hard to say the words and play their instruments at the same time, so either use the CD or say the poem yourself, but be prepared for the accompaniment to drown out the words somewhat!

Raindrops falling, raindrops falling…	*(xylophone(s)/glock(s). Slide a soft beater, or tap with a gently bouncing action from the smallest bar down to the largest.)*
Wind is stirring, wind is stirring…	*(cymbals. Play gently and repeatedly with a soft beater on the edge of the cymbal)*
Leaves are rustling, leaves are rustling…	*(shakers. If they have handles, turn them upside down and use a quick stirring action)*
Shutters banging, shutters banging…	*(loud clacks on any wooden instruments)*
Branches creaking, branches creaking…	*(scrapers or different wooden sounds)*
Rain and leaves are whirling, swirling…	*(xylophone(s)/glock(s), cymbals and shakers, not too loudly)*
Wind is really causing havoc…	*(all instruments loudly)*
	(Put your hands up to indicate to the children that they must stop playing and put the instruments very gently into their laps, so we don't get an extra clatter of sound as they all drop them on the floor!)
Wind has gone and all is calm…	*(Sit quite still and listen to the silence)*

Extension

- Tape your sound piece. Listen to the recording and talk about how you could improve the piece. Maybe some instruments could have been played more loudly/quietly. Perhaps the choice of instrument was not always appropriate.

Chapter 2
Sessions 11–20

Focus:
- Playing in time to a beat
- Listening for and recognising two different beats going on at the same time
- Clapping/playing/chanting a simple rhythm (ostinato)
- Following the leader

Session 11

Concept:
- Recognising the difference between two different beats heard separately – a medium speed and a faster speed

Theme: Well-known stories

Resource: CD track 10

The children are now used to playing the beat, but until now the emphasis has been on enjoyment and confidence. In these 10 sessions, work on critical listening to try and keep perfectly in time.

Do You Know the Story?
Tune: What Shall We Do With The Drunken Sailor?

1. I am a wood cut-ter chop-ping trees down, I am a wood cut-ter chop-ping trees down,

I am a wood cut-ter chop-ping trees down, do you know the sto-ry?

SHOUT: *Little Red Riding Hood*

2. I climbed a beanstalk and found the giant . . . (*Jack and the Beanstalk*)
3. I'm very sad 'cause I'm stuck here cleaning . . . (*Cinderella*)
4. I'm working hard on my house of bricks . . . (*Three Little Pigs*)
5. I'm spinning straw into gold by morning . . . (*Rumplestilskin*)
6. I am a prince cutting down this big hedge . . . (*Sleeping Beauty*)

- Talk about the different stories which feature in the song.
- Sing the song with the CD, track 10, shouting out the name of the story at the end of each verse. This is demonstrated on the CD at the end of verse 1.

Recognising two different beats in the song

- Sit in a circle and listen again to verse 1 of the CD. Don't sing this time. Can the children hear the beat and join in clapping? Encourage them to really focus and try to match the beat exactly. Now listen to verse 2 to see if anyone notices what is different about the beat. (It is faster).
- Listen to the rest of the song, but don't join in the clapping until you have clearly heard whether the accompanying beat is at a medium speed or a faster speed.
- Now try playing percussion instruments along with the CD, alternating the two beats from verse to verse. Encourage the children to look at you and copy *your* beat, in the same way that a member of an orchestra will follow the beat set by the conductor.

Extension

Miming other parts of the stories

- Choose one of the stories then ask the children to think of other parts of that story, for example the wicked fairy waving her wand in *Sleeping Beauty*, or the giant striding round in *Jack and the Beanstalk*. Show the children a mime of a part of a story you have discussed, and see if they can work out what it is.

Making up a new verse

- Now see if you can make up words for a new verse together, which will fit into the rhythm of the song and describe the mime. You might want to base your words on a completely different story. The children will not be able to manage without a great deal of help from you, but they will be developing an insight into how songs are formed by blending words, rhythm and tune. They should also get pleasure from the spontaneity of the invention of the words and the cleverness of the subsequent creation of a brand new verse in which they had a hand! The other skill here is making the words fit the tune really well, so nothing jars.

Session 12

Concept:

- Reinforcing recognition of two different beats – a medium speed and a faster speed

Theme: The Three Bears' House

Resource: CD track 11

The Three Bears' House

1. The three bears' house, it looks like this, it looks like this, it looks like this. The

three bears' house, it looks like this, in the mid - dle of the wood.

2. The smoke from the chimney curls like this . . . In the middle of the wood.
3. The flowers in the garden grow . . .
4. The gate in the garden opens . . .
5. The water fountain sprays . . .
6. The trees in the garden sway . . .
7. The little stream, it runs . . .

- Sing the song through making up actions to fit the words by drawing shapes in the air (e.g. the shape of a house for verse 1).

Three bears blindfold, whilst someone creeps to take an instrument

Who's been taking *my* instrument?

- Sit in a circle. Choose three contrasting instruments that you might associate with baby bear, mummy bear and daddy bear. Choose three children to be the three bears. They should sit in the middle of the circle, blindfold, each with their own instrument in front of them. Without saying the name, choose one child to creep into the middle of the circle, take one of the instruments and return to his/her place. The three bears, prompted by the teacher, should say 'Who's taken my instrument?' The child responsible says 'It was me!' Can any of the bears recognise whose voice that was? The child should then play the instrument. Whichever bear thinks it was his or her instrument should say 'It was mine!' (with prompting from the other two bears if necessary!) Choose three more bears and continue like this.

Recognising and clapping two different beats

- Sit in a circle and remind the children of how they heard two different beats in the song *Do You Know the Story?*
- Listen carefully to the CD (track 11) and ask the children to join in clapping with the beat as soon as they recognise it. On the CD the beat alternates between a medium one and a faster one just as it did in *Do You Know the Story?* but with this song the beat is slightly less obvious on the CD.

Extension

Playing two different beats

- Try the above activity with instruments. To make it more difficult, sing at the same time as playing.

Session 13

Concept:
- Using percussion to convey sound 'colour'

Theme: Sleeping Beauty

Resource: The story of Sleeping Beauty

Sleeping Beauty
- Read/tell the story of Sleeping Beauty.

Matching sounds to activities

First the activities…

- Talk about, then try out the following action ideas from the story:

    1. The loud, stamping cross footsteps of the wicked fairy
    2. The quiet tiptoeing footsteps of the Princess creeping round, exploring the Palace, on her fifteenth birthday
    3. The spinning wheel humming away
    4. The activity of all the busy servants working in the Palace, followed by the sudden cessation of activity at the moment when the Princess pricks her finger
    5. The Prince cutting the hedge down with his sword
    6. The celebrations following the marriage of the Prince and the Princess.

…now the instruments

- Sit down with the children and discuss which instruments would be appropriate for each activity, e.g. the hum of the spinning wheel might be represented by scraping finger nails gently round the skin of the drum, or by tapping a cymbal very quickly and quietly; the cutting down of the hedge could be conveyed by a mixture of wooden instruments and a cymbal played loudly.

Which activity goes with which sound?

- Ask the children to find a space of their own and get ready to listen to which instrument you play. They should then respond with the right activity.

Telling the story with instruments accompanying
- Next divide the children into six groups and give each group appropriate instruments (as discussed) so they are each representing one of the activities. Have the groups sitting in the order in which their sound will appear in the story. Make sure all the children are clear which part of the story they are accompanying. Now tell the story and allow 20–30 seconds playing time whenever you come to a part of the story to be conveyed by sound.

Extension

Telling the story with instruments
- Try the above activity, but make sure the groups are not sitting in order. The skill here is to make the association of story and sound quickly and accurately.

A game of signals and matching actions
- Decide together on specific shapes to represent some or all of the above activities, e.g. the spinning wheel might be represented by making a circular shape. Play the elimination game where you choose one of the instruments to play and the children must quickly respond with the relevant action.

Quick reactions – activity and silence

- Discuss with the children what kind of jobs the servants might do at the palace. In a space of their own the children should start doing their job with plenty of energy, while you play a tambourine quickly and loudly. They might pretend to be sweeping the floor or baking a cake, cleaning the windows or making the beds, but the moment you stop playing the tambourine they must freeze. Then when you start playing again they should resume work (a different job if they want). You might prefer to use music from a CD of your choice and pause it as the cue to stop work. The skill here is to respond quickly to the silence and to feel the contrast between activity and stillness.

Session 14

Concept:
- Introducing ostinato

Theme: Three Little Pigs

Resource: CD track 12

Three Little Pigs

2. Three little pigs, three little pigs,
   The second little pig built a house of twigs.
   What would you do, what would you do
   If the big bad wolf came chasing after pigs?

3. Three little pigs, three little pigs,
   The third little pig built a house of bricks.
   What would you do, what would you do
   If the big bad wolf kept getting up to tricks?

- On the CD (track 12) there is time between verses to clap the rhythm of the words 'big bad wolf' twice. Sing straight through the song with the claps between verses.

Introducing ostinato

First with actions…

- Listen to the first verse on the CD but don't sing this time. Just clap the 3 claps twice, exactly as you did before, at the end of the verse. Then carry on clapping the 3 claps throughout the whole of verse 2 while whispering the words 'big bad wolf'. A repeated idea like this, used to accompany a piece of music, is called an OSTINATO. At the end of verse 2, in place of the 2 lots of 3 claps, you give the rhythmic instruction 'Now stand up. Tap your heads!' The children should then tap their heads 3 times repeatedly throughout verse 3, while whispering the words 'big bad wolf'.
- Play the track again and accompany with the same ostinato throughout, but try different actions, such as alternating 3 knee pats with 3 toe pats: 'Knees, knees knees! Toes! Toes! Toes!'

…now with instruments

- Divide the class into three groups. Give each group instruments, making three different blocks of sound if possible. The first group should play the 'big bad wolf' ostinato throughout verse 1, the second group throughout verse 2 and the third group throughout verse 3, while the other two groups listen. Talk about this afterwards. Which group performed best? In what way was it best?

Taking turn to play the 'big, bad wolf' ostinato

Extension

- Try the activity above but sing at the same time!

Session 15

Concept:
- A more difficult ostinato

Theme: Sounds in the woods

Resource: CD track 13, the story *Good-night, Owl!* by Pat Hutchins

The Great, Big Wood

1. It's day time in the great big woods but the owl can't get to sleep._____ The bees buzz, 'buzz buzz buzz' but the owl can't get to sleep.

2. It's day time in the great big woods
   But the owl can't get to sleep.
   The squirrel cracks nuts, 'crack crack crack'
   But the owl can't get to sleep.

3. It's day time in the great big woods
   But the owl can't get to sleep.
   The woodpecker pecks, 'rat-a-tat-tat'
   But the owl can't get to sleep.

4. It's night time in the great big woods
   But the birds can't get to sleep.
   The owl screeches, 'T-wit-t-wit-t-woo!'
   But the birds can't get to sleep.

- This song is based on the story 'Good-night, Owl!' by Pat Hutchins. Read the story if possible then learn the song with the help of the CD (track 13).

Playing instruments on certain words

- Sit in a circle with the instruments in the middle and decide which instruments would best match the sounds e.g. 'buzz buzz buzz', conveyed in each verse. Divide the class into three groups, one for each of the first three verses, and give the instruments to each group according to what you have decided matches best. Tell the children they can all sing throughout, but only one group at a time will play their instruments, and only on the 'sound' words. Great restraint will have to be exercised to make sure the first group of children only play on the words 'buzz buzz buzz', the second group only on the words 'crack crack crack' and the third group only on the words 'rat-a-tat-tat'. Simply sing the last verse with no percussion accompaniment.

Accompanying with an ostinato

- Now practise chanting the words 'buzz buzz buzz' and 'crack crack crack' and 'rat-a-tat-tat'. Then re-play track 13 while clapping and quietly chanting the relevant ostinatos throughout the whole of the appropriate verse. This is a trickier exercise than for the previous song, because the tune of this song doesn't move so easily with the ostinato in places. Again simply sing the last verse.

Extension

- Divide the class into four groups, each group with different sounding instruments if possible, and take turns playing the ostinatos as above (one verse for each group). The last group should play very quietly while chanting the words *Good-night, Owl!*

Session 16

Concept:
- Concentrated focusing on/following a leader

Theme: Things that fly

Resource: Pictures of flying things (see second bullet point).

Look at the leader

- Divide the class into five groups, sitting as far apart from each other as possible. All the children must keep looking at you. Not as easy as it may seem! Looking at one of the groups, do an action, such as touching your head. This group must immediately touch their heads. Look at another group and fold your arms. This group should immediately fold their arms. Continue like this, switching from group to group rapidly, to help the children to simply get into the habit of keeping their eyes on you in the same way that members of an orchestra keep an eye on the conductor.

Which instruments match which flying things

- Sit in a circle with the instruments in the middle and talk about the following flying things: bees, butterflies, pigeons, helicopters, gnats. Show pictures if possible, then discuss the different sounds that each of these make. Which is the quietest, the noisiest, the biggest, the smallest? What about the type of flying action they have – smooth, flapping, fast, slow, hovering, fluttering? At this stage we are just looking for broad differences in order to choose the most appropriate instruments. You might decide on shakers for the bees, tambourines (just shaking the bells, not beating them) for the butterflies, drums for the beating of the pigeons' wings, wooden instruments for the clattering helicopters and finger chimes or gentle scraping sounds for the tiny hovering gnats.

Look at the conductor to know when to play

- Make sure the children are seated in five groups accordingly. You are going to be the conductor. They must try hard to keep looking at you all the time to see when to play, and just as importantly when not to play. Start by looking at one of the groups, while pointing and nodding vigorously! When you transfer your attention to another group, that group should play and the first group should stop, and so on. Don't worry about keeping to a beat. It is the maintaining of concentration that is the skill here.

- There are various ways of developing this activity:

  1. Gradually reduce the clues (pointing nodding etc) so that it is the children taking on the responsibility for themselves of knowing when to play. Eventually you should be able to simply look.
  2. Have a hand signal which tells a group to stop playing. Therefore, if you do not do the signal, that group should continue, so you might have up to five groups playing at once, and each group has no idea when it will be required to start or stop playing.

Look at the conductor to know when to sing

- Choose any popular song from the course so far and try the same activity as above but singing rather than playing. Only one group at a time should sing according to which group you are looking at.

Extension

- With the above activities, have a hand signal to show when you want the children to play/sing more loudly/more quietly.

Session 17

Concept:
- Following a leader
- Listening for two different beats going on at the same time

Theme: Animal noises

Resource: CD track 14; tape recorder and tape

Animal Noises

2. I'm purring in the sunshine . . .
   Yes I am a cat.

3. I'm hissing in the jungle . . .
   Yes I am a snake.

4. I'm clucking in the farmyard . . .
   Yes I am a hen.

5. I'm croaking on a lily pad . . .
   Yes I am a frog.

- Sing the song straight through with the CD, track 14.

Singing in two groups

- Divide the class into two groups. In verse 1, the first group should sing all but the last two words. Can the second group come in at exactly the right moment with the correct two words? In verse 2 the second group should sing the bulk of the verse and the first group come in at the right moment with the last two words. Continue like this swapping the groups for each subsequent verse.

Listening to two sounds at once

- Now divide the class into five groups. Each group should be allocated one of the following sounds: *Baa, miaow, hiss, cluck, croak*. Spend some time listening to each others' sounds to check they are clear and distinctive. Choose two groups to make their sounds repeatedly at the same time as each other. Could the children listening clearly hear both the sounds? Try that with different combinations of two groups.

Loud and quiet sounds – look at the conductor

- Now ask all the five groups to make their sounds at the same time quietly. If you point to one group, that group should change to making their sound loudly. The other four groups should still continue to make their sounds quietly, so they will be making a background 'wash' of sound. When your pointing finger moves to another group, the previous loud group should blend back into the background, so the new loud sound can come through. Continue like this.

Listening to two different beats played at the same time

- Sit in a circle and put on the CD track 14. Listen to verse 1 and all join in clapping with the medium speed beat when you can hear it clearly. Next listen to verse 2 and join in clapping with the subtle faster beat (exactly twice as fast as for verse 1).

- Pause the CD. Tell the children you are going to play them verse 3 on the CD then pause it again to ask them what beat they heard, the medium one or the fast one. (Loads of praise to anyone who recognised that they were both being played at the same time.) Both beats can also be heard in verses 4 and 5.

Extension

Playing two different beats at the same time

- Divide the class into two groups, each one sitting in a circle, and give each group contrasting sounding instruments. Play the CD, track 14. During verse 1, the first group should play in time with the medium beat, during verse 2 the second group should play in time with the faster beat. Then during the other three verses both groups should play their respective beats at the same time. *You* be the 'leader' in one circle and choose a reliable child from the other circle to be the leader. The other children should keep an eye on their respective leaders.

Session 18

Concept:

- Listening for and identifying two or three different sounds going on at the same time

Theme: More animal noises!

Resource: CD track 14; pictures of various animals – cat, duck, sheep, cow, dog, donkey, mouse

Animal Noises

- First sing the song (CD track 14).

Who made what noise?

- Sit in a circle and try out the following four contrasting animal noises: *quack, baa, miaow, moo*. Now ask one of the children to sit in the middle of the circle and hide their eyes or wear a blindfold. Point to one of the children in the circle who should make any one of the animal noises for a few seconds. The child in the centre must identify the animal that makes that noise and also identify which child made the noise. This is slightly more difficult than the game with the three bears (Session 12) because the child making the noise will most likely change the timbre of their natural voice to best imitate the animal.

Animals behind the screen

- Create a screen and ask two children to go behind it. Give each one a card with a picture of an animal on it. Ask the two children to make the noises on those cards at the same time, repeatedly and loudly. Can the other children identify *both* sounds?

Collecting animal noises

- The children should sit in a space of their own. Practise making the noise of a duck, all together, then the noise of a cow. Now choose two children to be collectors. Whisper to each of them which animal noise they will be listening for and collecting. Give them an allocated place in the room and tell that this is where they will be bringing 'their' animals when they have collected them. Ask the rest of the children to stand in a line so you can whisper to them 'quack' or 'moo'. (You might prefer to give a small card with a picture of the animal. The advantage of this is that they won't forget what noise to make, but the disadvantage is that the collector might be tempted to have a peep at the picture rather than do the collecting by using listening skills!) Ask the children to go back into spaces. At a given signal all the children should make their animal noise loudly and the two collectors should see how quickly they can collect all 'their' animals. To make more of a game of the activity, make sure you have even numbers of each animal and see which leader finishes collecting first.

Extension

- Try the activity 'Who made what noise?' with a wider choice of animals, and fewer repetitions of the noise. The extension here is that the child in the middle has to tune in more quickly.
- Try the 'Animals behind the screen' game with three or four noises going on simultaneously. The children could also make their noises very briefly.
- Try the 'Collecting animal noises' activity with three different noises and three leaders to collect.

Session 19

Concept:
- Following on
- A tricky ostinato

Theme: Food

Resource: CD track 15

What Do You Like to Eat?
Tune: A Sailor Went To Sea

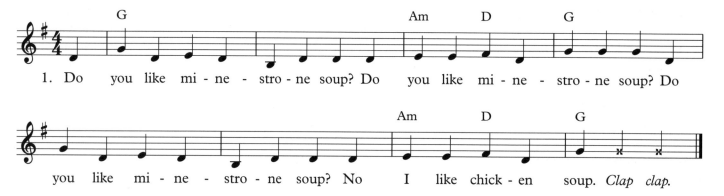

2. Do you like ham and mushroom pie? . . .
   No I like tuna pie.

3. Do you like peanut butter rolls? . . .
   No I like bacon rolls.

4. Do you like date and walnut cake? . . .
   No I like lemon cake.

5. Do you like choc'late chip ice cream? . . .
   No I like mint ice cream.

6. Do you like lemonade to drink? . . .
   No I like orange squash.

7. Do you like breakfast, lunch or tea? . . .
   I don't like one, I like all three!

- Sing the song through with the CD, track 15.
- The children will enjoy trying to sing the words at speed and doing the 2 claps at the end of each verse.
- Now try singing without the CD. Remind the children of the last line of verse 1, then sing the verse yourself, stopping immediately before the last line. Can the children come in at exactly the right moment with the right words for the last line? Try this with the other verses, reminding them of the last line beforehand each time.

Playing an ostinato
- Play the CD (verse 1 only) then pause it and ask the children if they heard the ostinato on the woodblock which went on throughout the verse. Listen again. The words CHICK-EN SOUP match the 3 beats of the ostinato. Play the CD again and whisper these words in time with the beat of the woodblock.
- Continue playing the rest of the song on the CD and whisper the ostinato TU-NA PIE throughout verse 2, BA-CON ROLLS throughout verse 3, etc. The extension here is that there is no help on the CD except in the first verse.

Extension

- Divide the class into two groups. One group should sing verses 1, 3, 5 and 7 while the other group says and/or claps the relevant ostinatos. In verses 2, 4 and 6 the groups should do the opposite. This activity can be done with or without the CD.

Session 20

Concept:

- Loud/Quiet
- Ostinato *and* a beat at the same time
- Working in a tight rhythmic framework

Theme: Keeping warm

Brr!

- Learn the following action rhyme. The children should stand in a space of their own The words dictate the actions for the verses. For the choruses the children should 'hug themselves' and 'twist' their upper bodies gently from side to side as though cold. Try to 'twist' with the beat, fitting 8 twists into the chorus each time, as shown below.

Brr!

CHORUS:
It's a <u>cold</u> cold <u>wind</u>, it's a <u>cold</u> cold <u>wind</u>.
We've <u>got</u> to keep <u>warm</u> cos it's a <u>cold</u> cold <u>wind</u>.

Stamp stamp stamp, stamp stamp stamp,
Jumping up and down and stamp stamp stamp.
CHORUS

Shake shake shake, shake shake shake,
Jumping up and down and shake shake shake.
CHORUS

Clap clap clap, clap clap clap,
Jumping up and down and clap clap clap
CHORUS

- Try saying the chorus quietly each time and the verse part loudly. Small children's voices tend to disappear when they are concentrating on actions, so this exercise takes concentration!

'It's a cold, cold wind'

A performance of the poem with a beat and an ostinato

- Divide the class into two groups, one sitting down with instruments, the other standing in spaces. The standing group should say the poem and do the actions as before. The sitting group should play the 3 beat ostinato, whispering the words 'stamp stamp stamp' throughout verse 1, 'shake shake shake' throughout verse 2, and 'clap clap clap' throughout verse 3. Repeat the activity swapping the groups over. Make sure the group with instruments plays very quietly indeed so as not to drown out the chanting groups.

Extension

- See if the instrumentalists can manage to play their ostinatos without whispering their words.

Working in a rhythmic framework

- Divide the class into three groups and give the first group instruments. Miss out the first chorus and start with verse 1. Group one should play the ostinato during this verse while the other two groups chant the words. As soon as verse 1 is finished all the children should move round one place, creeping on tiptoe and chanting the words of the chorus at the same time. They must then be sitting ready to chant verse 2 or play the ostinato. Move round again during the chorus between verses 2 and 3 and do verse 3 in the same way, so each group has a turn at playing the ostinatos, and the children are working in the rhythmic framework – i.e. the duration of the chorus is the exact length of time available in which to move round to the next place.

Chapter 3
Sessions 21–30

Focus:
- Tempo changes
- Identifying three different speeds of accompanying beat
- Developing rhythmic precision with two different beats/ostinatos at once
- Getting used to working in a rhythmic framework

Session 21

Concept:
- Slower/faster
- Working in a tighter rhythmic framework

Theme: Lazy Daisy

Resource: CD track 16

Lazy Daisy's Song

D   A7

1. This is La - zy Dai - sy's song, she does - n't jog, she strolls a - long.

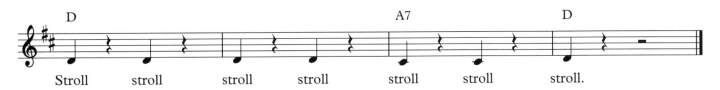

D   A7   D

Stroll   stroll   stroll   stroll   stroll   stroll   stroll.

2. This is Lazy Daisy's song,
   She doesn't jog she flops along.
   Flop flop flop flop flop flop flop.

3. This is Lazy Daisy's song,
   She doesn't jog she crawls along.
   Crawl crawl crawl crawl crawl crawl crawl.

- Stand still in spaces. With the CD (track 16) sing the first half of each verse, then stroll (walk slowly) during verse 1, flop (walk slowly flopped forwards) during verse 2, or crawl during verse 3, round the room with very slow steps in time with the beat of the words for the second half of the verse. On the CD there is no vocal line for verses 2 and 3, so the children will have to be quite sure of the words before they start.

Playing instruments on the action words

- Sit down in a circle, each child with an instrument. All join in playing instruments in time with the beat of the seven repeated action words at the end of each verse. The absence of a vocal line in verses 2 and 3 on the CD means that the children will have to follow the music carefully, imagining the words, to know when to come in with the instruments.

45

A performance of the song in a tight rhythmic framework

- Divide the class into three groups. Each group should have different sounding instruments, as usual. Stand to sing verse 1, all joining in playing the beat as before, on the repeated word 'stroll'. Then put the instruments down very quietly, and while singing the first part of verse 2, walk in time to the same slow beat to the next set of instruments, so all the groups have moved round one place. Pick up the instruments and be ready to play the slow beat on the different instruments with the repeated word 'flop'. This activity requires careful listening and great discipline to keep the 'swap over' confined exactly to the time frame of the first half of the verse. Repeat the procedure for verse 3. Again, the lack of vocal line on the CD for verses 2 and 3 means that the moment when the children should be ready to play their instruments, having swapped places, will not be flagged up so clearly.

Lazy Daisy goes for a walk

- Lazy Daisy is always trying to get fit. She sets off jogging with good intentions. The children can jog on the spot or if it's appropriate in your space, jog round the room. Make sure they know the difference between running and jogging. Demonstrate how less ground is covered with jogging. You accompany them with a drum beat.
- Now continue tapping the drum without a break, but slow down the tempo to a marching tempo. When the children have marched round for a short while, change your tempo to a slower one. The children should walk accordingly. The skill here is to concentrate hard on listening to the beat in order to notice the tempo changes. Encourage the children to keep an eye on you.

Extension

- Try the above activity, encouraging the children to respond by listening only, rather than keeping an eye on you.
- Sit in a circle, each child with an instrument. You are the leader now, so it is important that the children watch you carefully. Start off by playing a very slow steady pulse. The children should join in playing to match your beat. After about 10 seconds change the speed. You might like to follow a predictable pattern of tempo changes i.e. a slightly faster one, then an even faster one. Or you might prefer to change tempo without any pattern. Just make sure you keep to any one tempo for long enough to establish that beat.

Session 22

Concept:
- Matching a fast beat precisely

Theme: Zippy Zappy

Resource: CD track 17

Zippy Zappy

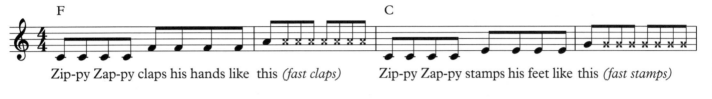

Zip-py Zap-py claps his hands like this *(fast claps)*   Zip-py Zap-py stamps his feet like this *(fast stamps)*

Zip-py Zap-py shakes his head like this *(fast head shakes)*   Zip-py Zap-py makes a shape like this   *(shape)*

- First sit in a circle and listen to the song on the CD, track 17. Notice how the claps and stamps and head shakes are fast but precisely even. Explain to the children that we are going to try to avoid messiness and keep to the beat neatly.
- Stand in the circle. First try out some interesting shapes that you can make easily. Now all sing the song through together with the actions, each child making a shape of their choice at the end. Ask a few children at a time to show the others, and talk about which children managed best to keep in time with the fast beat
- Without the CD, still standing in the circle, sing through in exactly the same way, only this time call out one of the children's names at the end of the last line: 'Zippy Zappy makes a shape like Jack!' Jack should then quickly make a shape, which all the other children should copy. Repeat with another child's name and so on.

Zippy Zappy goes to work

- Below are the musical signals *you* should make and the children's action responses.

Zippy Zappy is asleep	*the children curl up in a space of their own*
Finger chimes	*the children jump up at the sound of the alarm*
Shaker playing fast	*the children get dressed at top speed*
	(Until now all the children have been representing Zippy. Now choose one child only to represent him)
Shaker playing fast beats	*Zippy walks quickly to work (he is a wood cutter!)*
Drum playing slow beats	*Zippy stands still while the other children, who work as wood cutters with Zippy, swing their axes and chop the wood repeatedly very slowly in time to your beat*
Shaker playing fast beats	*Zippy is not impressed! He starts chopping quickly*
Drum playing fast beats	*The other workers are inspired by his speed and all join in at the same speed. They will have to use a much smaller action to accommodate the increased speed.*

- Repeat the activity with a different Zippy Zappy and a different job. It works best to choose a job which can be shown with a repeated action, such as cleaning windows, sweeping, cooking, hair dressing. You might like to practise some of these actions beforehand. Settle on the precise repetitive action for each job.

47

Extension

Same game, but now Zippy works as a player in a band!

• Give out a selection of percussion instruments. Tell the children that Zippy Zappy's job this time is as a player in a band. Do the waking up, getting dressed etc. as before, but when he gets to work, the rest of the band are playing their instruments rather than miming a job action, to the slow beat that you give them. Zippy then inspires them to play at a faster speed.

Session 23

Concept:
- Precision

Theme: Messy and neat

Messy Mop Top and Nathan Neat

- Explain to the children that Messy Moptop lives in a very untidy house with a big hairy gorilla called Gareth. They never clear up, so they can never find anything they need. Nathan Neat, on the other hand lives in a beautifully tidy flat with his cat, called Crispin.
- Show the pictures then say this little rhyme together:

Nathan Neat, Nathan Neat, Lives on neat and tidy street.	Nathan comes back home at five, Down the road and up the drive.
In a neat and tidy flat With his neat and tidy cat.	In the neat and tidy flat, Eats his tea and feeds the cat.
Nathan goes to work at eight, Never early, never late.	Now it's time to say goodnight. Nathan, watch the bugs don't bite!

- You say the first verse of the rhyme while clapping 8 even claps in time to the rhythm of the words. Without a break, the children should copy that. Try the other verses of the poem in the same way with no breaks in between. The children really have to stay focused to come in at exactly the right moment.

Messy and neat

- Tell the children that they can go round the room at any speed they want – walking very slowly, creeping, jogging, skipping, marching, striding and continually changing from one thing to another. But as soon as they hear you play the drum they must immediately start moving at the exact speed of the beat you are playing. (You can choose any speed you want.)
- Now repeat the activity, but beforehand tell the children that this time you are simply going to play 1 beat on the drum and that is the signal for them to start walking round at the same speed as each other. You will find that they settle, as if by magic, on a common speed. It is interesting to see which children are 'leaders' or 'speed setters' in this situation.
- Next try the same exercise with instruments. Sit in a circle and all play instruments at any speed, making a hubbub. But when you step into the middle of the circle and point to one of the children, that is the signal for all the children to adopt the speed set by the chosen child.

Extension

The messy and neat activity with instruments but no set speed

- Try the above activity with the instruments but don't point to anyone. As soon as the children see you in the middle they must try to conform to a single speed. Again, it is interesting to note which children are the 'leaders' or 'speed setters'!

Precision copying, one child at a time

- The children should sit in spaces. Crouch down beside one of them, and clap and say the first verse of the poem *Nathan Neat*. That child should clap and say it back to you. Now the children clap too while you walk in time to the beat to another child and crouch down. Say the second verse. The child claps and says it back to you. Continue with the rest of the poem in the same way. The extension here is that each child is taking on the responsibility of carrying the rhythm without the support of the others.

Session 24

Concept:
- Keeping to a slow beat in a rhythmic framework
- Internalisation

Theme: Elephants

Resource: CD track 18

Elephants

Plod plod, great feet plod
Elephants lumbering, lumbering.

Flap flap, big ears flap
Elephants listening, listening.

Whip whip, thin tails whip
Elephants watching, watching.

Curl curl, strong trunks curl
Elephants lifting, lifting.

Whoosh whoosh, long trunks whoosh
Elephants bathing, bathing.

Ssh! Ssh! Don't make a sound
Elephants slumbering slumbering.

- Sit in a circle and listen to the poem on the CD, track 18.

Plodding in time
- Play the track again and simply plod slowly and heavily round the room in time to the beat. Small children find it difficult to maintain slow, even steps. If any child is managing particularly well ask him/her to demonstrate.

Choosing sounds to match the action words
- Sit down in the circle again and put the instruments in the middle. Try to remember the various different sounds of the verbs used in the poem. Talk about which instruments would best convey these sounds. Divide the class into five groups – one to represent each verse, except the last - and distribute the instruments accordingly.

Accompanying with a slow beat
- Play track 18 again for each group to play to the slow beat throughout the relevant verse. Those children who are not playing should try to join in with the words. At the end, all whisper the words of the last verse, then sit perfectly still and listen to the silence for a few seconds.

Imitating the rhythm of the words (say and play)
- See if the children can manage to say the words of the first verse without the help of the CD. Now ask them to repeat that first verse while playing very quietly on their instruments *the precise rhythm that the words are making.* (So this is different from accompanying with a beat because they are making a sound for every syllable.)

Imitating the rhythm of the words without saying them
- Next, see if they can do the same exercise, only without vocalising the words. Tell them to try and say them inside their heads. It might help at first to form the words with the lips. All that will be heard is therefore the rhythm of the words on the instruments.

Extension

Imitating the rhythm of the words in groups
- Divide the class into four groups. Each group should have like sounding instruments. Keeping to the words of verse 1 only, one group at a time should play the rhythm of those words on their instruments, as above.
- Tape this then play it back and listen carefully to see which group sounded the clearest.

Session 25

Concept:
- 'Feeling' the time, space and energy of a slow speed
- A performance

Theme: An elephant dance

Resource: CD track 18; tape recorder and tape

Elephant's dance

Elephants

Plod plod, great feet plod
Elephants lumbering, lumbering.

Whip whip, thin tails whip
Elephants watching, watching.

Whoosh whoosh, long trunks whoosh
Elephants bathing, bathing.

Flap flap, big ears flap
Elephants listening, listening.

Curl curl, strong trunks curl
Elephants lifting, lifting.

Ssh! Ssh! Don't make a sound
Elephants slumbering slumbering.

Matching action words to dance movements

- Sit down and read the poem to the children again. Now talk about the action words. They have already shown plodding as a movement, by using heavy, thumping, slow footsteps. But what about 'thin tails whip'? Emulating the action of a tail need not necessarily represent this. It could be a fast flicking arm movement or a small rapid turn of the body from the waist up. The whoosh of the elephant's trunk might be a jump into a shape, flopping forwards from the waist up, or raising the arms then lowering them heavily, or lying down and raising and lowering a leg might represent the flap of the ear. Explore various movements then decide on one for each verse that contrasts well with the other chosen actions. Try also to vary the speed, shape and energy of the movement from verse to verse.

Combining instruments and movement – the grand performance!
- Divide the class into two groups. Play the CD, track 18, for one group to perform the dance, while the other group, divided into five smaller groups, plays the instruments chosen for each verse in the last session.

Extension

- To take this idea one step further, divide the class into three groups. Two of them will have the same function as for the previous activity, and the third should chant the words of the poem, instead of using the CD.
- Try taping the results the listen and talk about the recording. Could the words and the instruments be clearly heard at all times?

Session 26

Concept:
- 'Feeling' a slow speed
- Slower/faster

Theme: Our school train
Resource: CD track 19

The Dingleden Train

- First sit down in a space to learn the song, which is sung through twice and fades out on the third time through, on the CD. Substitute the name of your school/playgroup/nursery for Dingleden.
- Next stand up and try walking round very slowly in time to the music as you sing. Get used to singing this song without the help of the CD
- Now to make the train. You be the leader at first. The children should stay still and sing the song repeatedly, nice and slowly. When you tap a child gently on the head (s)he must 'join on' behind you. I usually tell the children to place their hands lightly on the waist of the person in front. (Adapt that for joining on to you!) Tap a child every few seconds, so it takes between five and ten run-throughs of the song to have all the children joining on, forming the train. As the leader, make sure you snake about, rather than going round and round in a circle. This is a skill in itself. Encourage a slow rhythmic walk in time to the beat, though it is not easy walking along one behind the other like this. So as long as the children are not dragging each round at break neck speed, don't worry about keeping in time!
- At the very end, when all the children have formed the train, see if you can gently turn it into a circle. Show the children how the leader should cut across the circle to join on to the child at the back, rather than chasing round and round! I will always remember one little boy in my class, who, when tapped on the head said to the leader, 'No, I want to be the dump'. As the song continued I gave these words some thought and realised that he had misunderstood the meaning of the word 'tip'… 'till the top meets the tip' (!!)
- Now repeat the activity, choosing one of the children to be the leader.

Individual trains
- In a space of their own, the children are all going to listen to your tambourine, or better still, sandblocks. Play very slowly at first, to cue the trains to start moving. The children should take tiny shuffling footsteps and emulate the train in the traditional way with their hands making circles at their sides. As you play gradually faster, so the children must shuffle along more quickly, but always listening for the moment when you start to slow down again, and finally stop. Try this in two groups. One group simply watches the other and vice versa so the children can observe who was a particularly good-at-listening train!

The Dingleden Train

Extension

The Dingleden dance

- Try the following dance when the circle has been formed at the end of the 'Dingleden Train' activity and song: all hold hands and do 8 gallops to the left, then 8 to the right. This will take a great deal of practice to make sure that everyone knows which way to go, and to keep the circle under control. I always tell the children not to 'stretch' the circle. At the end of the gallops, let go of hands and do 2 slow stamps, then 2 claps and finish with 3 head taps and 3 floor pats. These actions will fit into one sing-through of the song, so you might like to try it with the CD.

Session 27

Concept:
- Recognising three different speeds of beat

Theme: Transport

Resource: CD track 20

Lots of Forms of Transport
Tune: Bobby Shaftoe

CHORUS: You may want to tra-vel quick-ly, you may want to tra-vel slow-ly, you may want to

make a jour-ney in a fer-ry boat. 1. Boats go sail-ing on the sea, boats go sail-ing
2. in the Eu-ro-star.
3. in a Boe-ing jet.
4. on a mo-tor-bike.

on the sea, boats go sail-ing on the sea, they're a form of trans-port.

CHORUS:
You may want to travel quickly,
You may want to travel slowly,
You may want to make a journey in the Eurostar.

2. Trains go whizzing on the rails
   Trains go whizzing on the rails
   Trains go whizzing on the rails
   They're a form of transport

CHORUS:
You may want . . .
. . . in a Boeing jet.

3. Planes go soaring in the air . . .

CHORUS:
You may want . . .
. . . on a motor bike.

4. Bikes go roaring on the road . . .

- Start to learn the song with the CD track 20. There are a lot of quick words to fit in. This, in itself, is quite a task.

Recognising and clapping the three different speeds of beat

- Now play the CD again and ask the children to listen very carefully to the first chorus and verse. They should join in clapping with the accompanying medium beat as soon as they hear it.
- Pause the CD at the end of verse 1 and tell the children to get ready to listen again. Can they identify and join in clapping with the faster beat that runs through the music of the second chorus and verse on the CD?
- Pause the CD again and warn the children that the beat for the next chorus and verse will seem much slower. See if they can join in, in the same way, with this third chorus and verse on the CD.
- Pause the CD again and tell the children that all three speeds – slow, medium and fast – accompany the last chorus and verse. Close your eyes and simply listen to the CD. The slowest speed is the most difficult to detect.

- Now play the whole track, accompanying the first chorus and verse by clapping a medium beat, the second chorus and verse by clapping a fast beat, the third chorus and verse with a slow beat and the fourth chorus and verse with any of those 3 beats. You might find that all the children conform to the same beat as each other, but be prepared to dole out lots of praise if 2, or better still all 3 beats come through in the clapping!

Extension

Individual trains with instruments

- Sit in a circle. Each child should have an instrument. Try the activity 'Individual Trains' from the last session, but in reverse. You be the train going very slowly at first then gradually more quickly and so on. The children must watch you carefully and play faster when you go faster and more slowly when you slow down. So you are still the leader in terms of setting the tempo changes.

Session 28

Concept:
- Fast/Medium/Slow
- Working with three different beats (and no clues on the CD!)

Theme: More transport

Resource: CD track 20

Lots of Forms of Transport
- First sing the song through with the CD, track 20.

Mixing up three pulses randomly – clapping
- Now play the CD again. Start by playing claves in time with the fast pulse (i.e. 1 beat per syllable.) Ask the children to join in clapping at the same speed, not too loudly. They should watch and listen to you all the time. Warn them that you might suddenly change speed at any time and that they must be ready to change too. Make the change whenever you want to, (not necessarily at the end of a verse or chorus), but make sure your beat is exactly twice as slow as the previous one and falls on every other syllable. When the children have adapted to this speed, change to an even slower pulse, your beats falling on every fourth syllable. If the song is not finished, change your beat back to one of the other two speeds for the children to copy. The extension here is that you are all finding your own pulse without the help of the CD (in fact *despite* the CD!)

Mixing up three pulses randomly – actions
- Now try the same activity but with actions. The children should stand in a space of their own and be ready to copy your action, making sure they are exactly matching the speed. Play the CD and start with a small action, such as opening and closing fists, for the quickest pulse, a medium action, such as patting knees or marching on the spot for the medium pulse and a big action such as raising both arms at the sides, then lowering them (this comprises 2 beats) for the slowest pulse.

Extension

Individual trains with instruments
- Repeat the activity from the extension section of the last session, but choose a child to be the train setting the speed changes.

Session 29

Concept:
- Mixing up three beats and an ostinato

Theme: Alternative transport!

Resource: CD track 20; pictures of a pram, a donkey roller-blades and a donkey

Lots of Forms of Transport

- First sing through the song with the CD track 20. Play the three different speeds of beat on instruments to accompany.

The syllable game

1) Forming four groups

- You will need pictures of a pram, a donkey, roller blades, and a helicopter. Those words have one, two, three and four syllables respectively. Stick the pictures up in four different places in your room.
- Gather the children around you and practise clapping and saying each word, explaining the difference between them, counting the syllables etc, until you are sure the children understand and can recognise which is which.
- Now say one of the children's names and tap one of the four words on your claves. The child must go to the right place.
- Continue like this, aiming to finish up with four roughly equally sized groups.

2) Playing instruments in groups

- Look at the illustration below, which shows how the four different words can be fitted rhythmically into each other and also into the song. This is simply another way of showing the three different speeds of beat in the music, except for ROLL-ER BLADES, which is an ostinato because it mixes two different speeds of beat in one little figure.

You		may	want	to	tra	vel	quick	ly
Don	-	key			Don	-	key	
He	-	li	-	cop	-	ter	He - li - cop - ter	
Pram					Pram			
Roll	-	er	blades		Roll	-	er	blades

- Give all the children an instrument, making sure that you don't have more than one type of sound in any one group.
- Play the CD, track 20. All the children should tap DON-KEY very quietly and evenly on their instruments during the first chorus. Then let the group sitting by the picture of the donkey continue to tap the word throughout verse 1, while the other groups whisper the word repeatedly.
- All tap the word HE-LI-COP-TER quietly and evenly throughout the second chorus. Then let the group sitting by the picture of the helicopter continue to tap the word throughout verse 2 while the other groups whisper the word.
- Continue like this – verse 3 = PRAM and verse 4 = ROLL-ER BLADES.

Extension

- Choose any two groups to try tapping their repeated words at the same time.

Session 30

Concept:
- 'Feeling' groups of four equal beats

Theme: Weather

Resource: CD track 21 tape recorder and tape

The Weather Wonder Band with instruments

1. When the hail beats down, when the hail beats down, when the
hail beats down in the wea - ther won - der-land, we can beat the drum, we can
beat the drum, we can beat the drum in the wea - ther won - der band.

2. When the wind shakes the trees . . .
   We can shake our tambourines . . .

3. When the sun comes out . . .
   We can play our bells . . .

4. When the ice goes drip . . .
   We can tap our claves . . .

- First learn the song. There are lots of words to fit in – a skill in itself. Accompany verse 1 with drums, verse 2 with tambourines, verse 3 with Indian bells or finger-chimes and verse 4 with claves.

Putting sets of four actions with the song

- All stand in a space. Try out the following action sequence to a slow beat: 4 head taps, 4 claps, 4 knee pats, 4 floor taps (using both hands). Play the CD track 21. Fit the actions into verse 1.
- Can the children help you to make up another action sequence for verse 2? Repeat the verse 1 sequence during verse 3, and the verse 2 sequence during verse 4.

Make up your own piece of music on the theme of weather

- Use the weather ideas from the song. Discuss which would be the best instruments for hail, wind etc. Also consider whether the four different weather ideas will simply appear one after the other, or will they overlap in some way? What about speed? All the same? Varying according to the weather? What about dynamics? Which weather should sound the loudest? Remember you are using the instruments to convey sounds in an expressive way, rather than to accompany a beat.

Extension

- Tape your piece and discuss the recording afterwards. If you shut your eyes can you really imagine the hail, the wind, the sun and the ice? Could you improve on the piece if you tried it again?
- Go back to the activity 'Putting sets of four actions with the song'. Try doing the actions at double the speed, and fitting two whole sequences into each verse. This will be fast, so choose small actions.

Chapter 4
Sessions 31–40

Focus:
- High/Low
- Getting higher/lower
- Consolidating two beats at a time and ostinato
- Precision
- Performance

Session 31

Concept:
- Performance
- Precision

Theme: Minibeasts

Resource: CD track 22

My Minibeast Friends

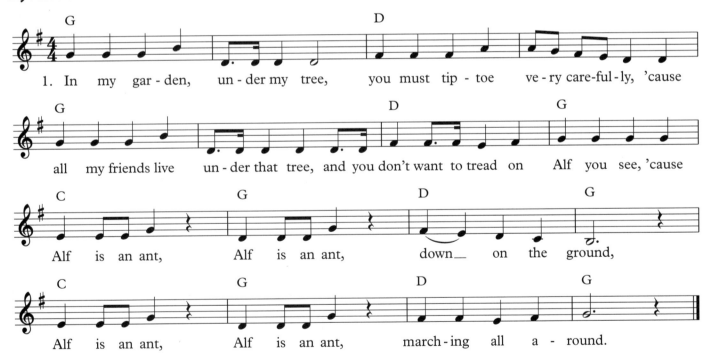

2. Will is a woodlouse . . .
   Creeping all around.

3. Ben is a beetle . . .
   Beetling all around.

4. Sid is a snail . . .
   Strolling all around.

59

- The children should stand in a space to sing the song. They should stand quite still for the first part of each verse, then do the following actions for the second part...

Alf is an ant, Alf is an ant	*clap to the left, then to the right, and repeat. (i.e. 4 even beats)*
Down on the ground	*point down as you slowly crouch down, till your fingers touch the ground*
Alf is an ant, Alf is an ant	*repeat the 4 claps*
Marching all around	*4 marches on the spot*

The last line of each verse each has a different action each time:

Creeping	*4 tiptoe steps forwards*
Beetling	*take tiny shuffling steps*
Strolling	*4 slow, casual steps*

A performance of the song

- This is quite a long song with several action elements, and so it lends itself well to a performance. You don't need an audience to do a performance(!) – just make a big thing out of asking the children to stand up very straight, and concentrate hard on what comes next. The words 'Pretend we're on a stage with lots of people watching who will only clap if we do it very well' help to convey the idea that this is special!

Appraising the performance

- In the extension part of the last session (*The Weather Wonderband*) the children's critical appraisal skills were developed by listening to the recording of the composition and considering how to improve it. Continue that idea here by asking the children if they were ready to march or stroll, for example, and if they were clapping precisely on the beat and singing their best.

Marching, creeping, beetling, strolling with the beat

- Now play the CD and simply march to the beat during verse 1, tiptoe round to the beat during verse 2, 'beetle' round with tiny shuffling footsteps to the fast beat during verse 3, and walk/stroll round to the slow beat during verse 4. If any children are keeping in time particularly well ask them to demonstrate, then encourage the rest of the children to join in, trying to match those children's steps.

Extension

Another performance of the song

- Divide the class into two groups. One group should play instruments in time with the marching beat during verse 1, the quieter beat, at the same speed, during verse 2, the fast beat during verse 3 and the slow beat during verse 4. The other group should sing and do the actions as before. Then swap the two groups round.

Session 32

Concept:

- High/Low
- Two beats at a time

Theme: More minibeasts

Resource: CD track 22

My Minibeast Friends

- Sing through the song with the actions.

Two beats at a time

- Divide the class into two groups. All of the children should have instruments. Play the CD and ask group one to play the marching beat during the first verse and group two to play a slow beat during the second verse. During the third verse, see if both groups can play their beats at the same time, then swap to the other group's beat during the fourth verse. The extension is that the accompanying beats being played are not the same as those on the CD.

High and low notes on the xylophone

- Talk about the difference between flying and non-flying insects. Think of as many different insects and minibeasts as you can. The flying ones can go up high in the air, the non-flying ones stay down on the ground. Ask the children to listen to you playing some notes on the xylophone. Play only the longer bars at the bottom and tell the children that these are the low notes, down at the bottom of the xylophone, like the insects that crawl around down on the ground. Then play the smaller bars at the top of the xylophone and tell the children that these are the insects flying high up in the air.
- Put the xylophone where the children can't see it and play a few notes, either the high ones or the low ones. If the children think you played the low ones they should curl up in a ball, being one of the non-flying insects; if they think you played the high ones, the should stand on tiptoe and stretch their wings like an insect flying up in the air.
- If this is easy add a third pitch by playing the middle notes on the xylophone. When they hear these notes the children should simply stand normally (i.e. without stretching their arms).

Extension

High can be Loud or Quiet; Low can be Loud or Quiet

- Reinforce the concept Loud/Quiet in context with this new concept High/Low with the following game. Tell the children that now they are listening for four different possible sounds, two of them will be high and two will be low. One of the high ones will be exactly the same as for the previous activity, and the other is a helicopter, which is also high, but is very noisy. One of the low ones will be exactly the same as for the previous activity but the other will be a racing car, which is also low, but is very noisy too. This means that the children must be listening to see, not only if you play high or low, but if you play loudly or quietly. To show the helicopter sound they could stand with one arm stretched up high and one finger pointing up and making a little circle in the air to represent the propeller. To show the racing car, they could simply pretend to be holding the steering wheel. Leave the middle pitch out and try an elimination game.

Session 33

Concept:
- Higher and lower

Theme: Even more minibeasts

Resource: CD track 23

Felicity Fly
Tune: For He's A Jolly Good Fellow

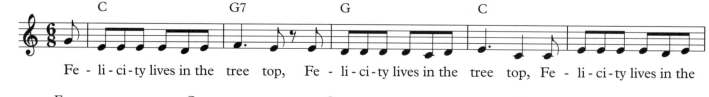

Fe - li - ci - ty lives in the tree top, Fe - li - ci - ty lives in the tree top, Fe - li - ci - ty lives in the

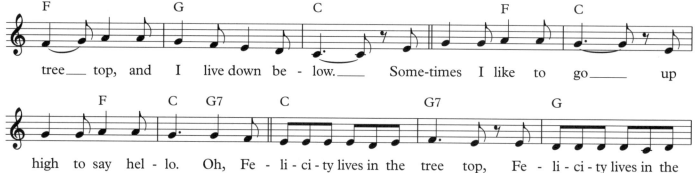

tree ___ top, and I live down be - low. ___ Some-times I like to go ___ up

high to say hel - lo. Oh, Fe - li - ci - ty lives in the tree top, Fe - li - ci - ty lives in the

tree top, Fe - li - ci - ty lives in the tree ___ top, and I live down be - low. ___

- Sit down to sing the song. Talk about which insect Felicity Fly's friend (who lives 'down below' in the song) might be – an ant or a beetle a caterpillar or a woodlouse who goes crawling up a tree to see her? Or is it a ladybird who likes to *live* on the ground then fly up to see her?

Children stretched up

Crawling/flying up and down the tree

- Play all the notes from the bottom of the xylophone to the top. Actually tap each one, rather than sliding your beater up them. Tell the children that this is the insect crawling (or flying if you play the ascending notes quickly) up to see Felicity Fly. Now play the same notes descending and tell the children that this is the insect coming back down to the ground.

- Now put the xylophone out of the children's view. The children should stand in a space and get ready to listen. Play the notes very slowly either in the ascending or the descending order. As soon as the children think they know which way you are going they should either crouch down and start to grow, finishing by raising their hands up high, OR they should start by stretching up tall and slowly lower their hands then their bodies until they are crouching down low. They should stay in their final position while you tell them which ones were right. Those who were not right are 'out'. Continue like this. The extension here is that children find it harder to recognise notes which are *getting* higher/*getting* lower than notes which are simply high or low.

Insect names with different numbers of syllables

- Try the activity (similar to the one in session 29) where the children have to listen to how many syllables there are in various insect words. Listen to the number of syllables in the following insect names: ANT, BEE-TLE, BUT-TER-FLY, CAT-ER-PIL-LAR. Divide the class into four groups, one to represent each insect. Give each group instruments. If you tap 1 tap, the ants should play and say their word repeatedly, 2 taps – the beetles, 3 – the butterflies and 4 – the caterpillars.

Extension

- All the children must watch you carefully. Point to two of the groups. Those two must play and say their insect words repeatedly and quietly at the same time. Keep mixing up the combinations.

Session 34

Concept:
- High/Low
- Recognising more subtly different rhythmic patterns

Theme: Yet more minibeasts

Resource: CD track 23

Felicity Fly
- First sing through the song.

Names with more complicated, less distinguishable sounds
- Introduce the following four characters – Alison Ant, Sid Snail, Bethany Butterfly, Walter Woodlouse. Tap these four different names a few times on a drum, while saying them to fit the beat, and making sure the children can hear the difference between them.
- Divide the class into four groups and whisper one of these names to each group. They should practise clapping and whispering their given minibeast name so that the other groups cannot hear. Then practise clapping it while keeping their lips still and only saying the word inside their heads.
- Now let each group take turns clapping their minibeast name repeatedly to see if anyone from one of the other groups can guess which one it is. Remind the children of the four possibilities before the clapping starts. It will be easy to guess the last group's minibeast by process of elimination, so whisper one of the other three to them for the purposes of the activity.

A game recognising high/medium/low notes using the same names
- Keep the same minibeast name for each group. Tell the children that you are going to play one of these names on your xylophone. You might play it at a high, a medium or a low pitch. If you play e.g. Alison Ant at a low pitch, then that group should all curl up in little ball shapes. If you play one of the four names at a high pitch, the relevant group should stand up and stretch their arms high. Or if you play a name at the medium pitch, the relevant group should simply stand up. See how quickly the children can recognise and respond to these musical signals.

Extension

Playing two names at the same time, watching the conductor
- Remind yourselves of the extension for the previous session. The object of the exercise was for all the children to watch you carefully to see whose turn it was to play and say their minibeast name. This time the names are longer and there is another extension too. You are going to do the activity, without any break. This means that the children must watch your pointing fingers the whole time to see if you have stopped pointing to them and have changed to another group. Sometimes you might change both the groups at the same time, other times you might allow one group to keep playing while you change the other one.

Session 35

Concept:
- Getting higher/getting lower
- Performance

Theme: Boogie Bugs

Resource: CD track 24

Boogie Bugs

1. Clap your hands for the boo-gie bugs, boo-gy-ing right down on the ground.

Clap your hands for the boo-gie bugs, boo-gy-ing a-round and a-round. Well you

boo-gie to the left, boo-gie to the right, boo-gy-ing with-out a sound.

2. Swing your hips for the boogie bugs . . .
3. Tick tock heads . . .
4. Jump jump jump . . .
5. Pat your knees . . .
6. Stamp stamp stamp . . .

- Sing the song through with the actions. Most of them are self explanatory. Point down slowly on 'down on the ground', turn round on 'boogying around and around', sideways gallop on 'boogie to the left – boogie to the right'. Choose your own action(s) for the last line. Throughout the dance/song, keep a constant 'wiggling' of the hips going, so that it feels like a real dance and not just a set of actions.

Eight body positions to represent ascending notes
- On your xylophone play very slowly from a low C to a high C. You will be playing 8 notes. Here are the growing actions that the children will do at the same time:

  1. Curl up in a ball
  2. Kneel with bottom on feet
  3. Kneel up
  4. Kneel on one leg
  5. Stand but bent over
  6. Stand up straight
  7. Put hands on shoulders
  8. Stretch arms up high.

These actions should give the children the feel of getting higher. Now reverse them for getting lower.

From high to low

Going up or going down?

- Ask the children to sit in a space of their own and close their eyes. Tell them to listen to see if you play notes going up (getting higher), or going down (getting lower). Play the 8 notes quite quickly either ascending or descending. They should point up or down to show you what they think. The extension here is that now the children have only 8 notes in which to judge if those notes ascend or descend.

Extension

- Try a performance of *Boogie Bugs* with some of the children playing instruments to two different beats, either at the same time as each other, or one after the other, while the others sing and do the actions.

Session 36

Concept:
- High/Medium/Low
- Performance
- An ostinato and a beat at the same time

Theme: The jungle

Resource: CD track 25; tape recorder and tape

Jing-a-jing-a-jungle

1. Jing-a-jing-a-jungle, jing-a-jing-a-jungle
   Caterpillars, caterpillars, crawling through the trees.
   Jing-a-jing-a-jungle, jing-a-jing-a-jungle
   Sing a song of jungalese.

2. ...Butterflies, butterflies, flying through the trees...

3. ...Monkeys, monkeys, leaping through the trees...

4. ...Snakes, snakes, gliding through the trees...

- Learn the chant all together with the CD.

A grand, four-part performance of the chant
- We are going to build up to the following performance of the chant with the children in four groups. The preparation for this performance follows in the next bullet point.

In verse 1:
Group 1: chant the words
Group 2: play the ostinato *jing-a-jing-a-jungle*
Group 3: play the rhythm of the word *caterpillars*
Group 4: crawl slowly round being the caterpillars

In verse 2:
Group 2: chant the words
Group 3: play the ostinato *jing-a-jing-a-jungle*
Group 4: play the rhythm of the word *butterflies*
Group 1: fly round being the butterflies

(Continue swapping round in the same way for verses 3 and 4.)

Four groups

Preparing for the above performance

- Take verse 1. There are four tasks involved – one for each group. Rather than trying out all four at once, just take two of them. So divide the class into two groups and see if they can manage verse 1 with two of the elements. Then try the same verse with another combination of two elements. Keep working like this, building up to having all four elements going on at the same time.

Extension

High/medium/low voices

- Sit in a circle. Practise speaking at three different pitches. We are going to call your normal speaking voice *medium pitch*, speaking in a high, squeaky voice, *high pitch*, and speaking in a deep, growly voice, *low pitch*.
- Try this activity now. Play one of the long songs such as *We're Going on a Holiday* (track 4 on the CD) while passing a drum round the circle. Pause the CD every so often. Whoever is holding the drum at that time should say their name in one of the three pitches and the others all then repeat it at the same pitch. This helps children to feel the range of their voices and make the connection between high, medium and low sounds.

Session 37

Concept:
- Getting lower/getting higher with fewer notes
- Feeling sets of four beats

Theme: Church bells

Resource: CD track 26

The Bell Ringer

- For this song we are trying to hear the difference between two sounds that are fairly close together in pitch, so we are demanding a great degree of aural discrimination. Look at the little illustrations on the song for the actions. Explain about ringing church bells, and how you need to pull the rope down then let it go back up again. The song is sung through just once on the CD.

Getting lower/getting higher with only 5 notes

- Ask the children to sit in a space of their own and listen to your xylophone. Play the following descending 5 notes: G F E D C and then the same 5 notes, ascending. Tell the children that the descending notes are pulling the rope down, and the ascending notes are letting the rope go back up again. Ask them to stand up and do those two actions repeatedly to match your playing.

Making a game of it

- Now ask them to sit down and close their eyes. Play the 5 notes, either ascending or descending. Can the children tell you which one you played? If they thought you played the notes descending they should pull the bell rope down and stay at the bottom. If they thought you played them ascending, they should reach up high, holding the rope. The extension here from the previous session is that now the children have only 5 notes with which to judge whether those notes were ascending or descending. Again, make an elimination game out of this if you want.

Singing *The Bell Ringer* with a few pitched notes to accompany

- If you have any chime bars, wonderful! Give a C and a G to one of the children and a pair of finger chimes to another of the children. Otherwise, use a glockenspiel instead of the chime bars. Everyone sing the song with the actions. When you come to the words 'High, low, high, low' the child with the glockenspiel should beat the notes G C G C. (See the section 'Tips when playing instruments' in the introduction.) At the end of the song the child with the finger chimes should play 4 beats in time with the words 'swing, swing, swing, swing.'
- Try the same activity with two different children playing, and so on.
- Let the children take turns in pairs. One of the pair plays the C, the other the G in time to the slow beat of the music throughout. Who can match the piano on the CD the best?

Extension

Sets of 4 claps

- Sit in a circle and take turns to do 4 claps each round the circle in time to the slow beat of the music of the CD (track 27).

Session 38

Concept:

- Going up and down (only 5 notes)
- Performance; feeling sets of four beats

Theme: Actions

Resource: CD track 27

Down on the Ground

2. . . . slowly put your hands upon the ground.
3. . . . slowly put your knees upon the ground.
4. . . . slowly put your bottom on the ground.
5. . . . slowly put yourself upon the ground.

- First play the CD, track 27 and learn the following actions:

Keeping to the beat, walking here and there	*Take 4 slow steps in a square (or 2 forwards and 2 back.)*
Shake your fingers high up in the air, and then you	*Raise both hands up high and shake fingers*
Jump and jump and jump without a sound,	*4 jumps*
Roll your shoulders round and round and round, and	*roll shoulders*
Jump and jump and jump without a sound, and then you	*4 jumps*
Slowly put your fingers on the ground	*go down to the ground in a distinctive, dancy way, wiggling your hips to the beat.*
(With each successive verse you finish up with more of you on the ground!)	

A game of recognising 5 pitched notes getting higher/lower

- Sit down and talk about the last little bit of the tune of the song. Can the children tell that it is the same 5 notes going down that they heard in the last session when they played the game of recognising whether the notes went up or down? Here the rhythm is a skipping rhythm though. Play G F E D C so it skips like the last bit of this song, while singing the words 'fingers on the ground'. Then play it in reverse while singing the words 'fingers in the air'. Do this a few times to get used to the different sounds of ascending and descending notes. Now play the same game as before, where you conceal the xylophone from view and play one or the other. The children must respond with the right action.

Extension

Sets of 4 actions (slow then fast)

- Building on the extension from the last session, try out plenty of ideas of sets of 4 actions. Include original ones such as pretending to strum a guitar, opening and closing fists, doing a sawing action. Either ask the children to simply copy you as you improvise actions in sets of 4, or work out a sequence of 4 sets of 4 actions, and keep repeating the sequence with track 27 of the CD. At first keep with the slow beat and then see what happens if you do the actions twice as fast, following the fast beat.

Session 39

Concept:
- Recognising three different pitches

Theme: The seasons

Resource: CD tracks 28 and 29

Back Another Day

1. 'Good morn - ing Ra - chel Ro - bin, what have you got to say?' 'I'm here be-cause it's win - ter, it's a win - ter's day to - day.' But when the win - ter's o - ver and spring is on its way, it's good - bye to Ra - chel Ro - bin, she'll be back an - o - ther day.

2. 'Good morning Charlie Chicken, what have you got to say?'
   'I'm here because it's springtime, it's a springtime day today.'
   But when the spring is over and summer's on its way,
   It's goodbye to Charlie Chicken, he'll be back another day.

3. 'Good morning, Chelsea Chaffinch, what have you got to say?'
   'I'm here because it's summer, it's a summer's day today.'
   But when the summer's over and winter's on its way,
   It's goodbye to Chelsea Chaffinch, she'll be back another day.

4. 'Good morning, Sophie Spider, what have you got to say?'
   'I'm here because it's autumn, it's an autumn day today.'
   But when the autumn's over and winter's on its way,
   It's goodbye to Sophie Spider, she'll be back another day.

- First try the actions with the CD, track 28. See the diagrams on the song for the different parts of the body that you have to touch. These are directly related to the pitch of the notes in the song. Can the children hear that the line 'But when the winter's over' is the highest part of the song? Make sure they understand the connection between the higher and lower parts of the body and the higher and lower parts of the song.
- Now sit down in four groups. Tell the groups that they are representing Rachel Robin (winter), Charlie Chicken (spring) Chelsea Chaffinch (summer) and Sophie Spider (autumn). All the children should sing the question at the start of each verse, then the relevant group should sing the answer, and all the children should then finish off the verse each time.

Listening to high sounding and low sounding instruments

- Listen to track 29 of the CD. Have a discussion about the three little extracts here. The instrument that plays the first extract is the violin, a high member of the string family, the second extract is played by the bassoon, which is a low member of the woodwind family, and the third is played by the treble recorder, which is bigger than the familiar descant recorder and also belongs to the woodwind family.
- Talk about the extracts. Which instrument played high notes? And low notes? Were the extracts Loud/Quiet, Fast/Slow, Smooth/Bouncy? How did they make you feel? Did they remind you of anything?
- This track provides you with a starting point for listening to other extracts of music and discussing the music afterwards. Try to get hold of pictures of the instruments – or better still, do you know anyone who might come in and give a demonstration of live music?

Extension

A performance of the song *Back Another Day*

- Divide the class into three groups:

  Group 1: a large singing group, including four children to represent the four characters in the song.
  Group 2: a percussion group, playing the beat during the first half of the song
  Group 3: a percussion group playing the beat during the second half of the song.

- Next time you try it through, swap the groups around. (The extension here is that the children are having to come in at a less obvious place in the music)

Session 40

Concept:
- Performance with High/Low, Fast/Slow and Loud/Quiet

Theme: Music based on a story

Resource: Tape recorder and tape

Making up a piece of music based on a story

- Previously when we have made up a composition, the starting point has been a poem. You might have a favourite poem which you would like to use, or you might know a simple story, whose plot line provides inspiration.

The Enormous Turnip

- This is just one of many stories (traditional and modern) which lend themselves well to musical adaptation. In the story we see the turnip growing more and more day by day and outgrowing all the other turnips. Then a man tries to pull it out, but is unsuccessful so his wife joins him, then his children, then various animals join in one at a time. It is the little mouse at the end of the line that adds that tiny bit of strength necessary to pull out the turnip. Everyone falls over. At the end, the family have a turnip feast!

One way of translating that story to instruments

- All the instruments play together to start with, but very very quietly. They then play gradually more and more loudly to convey the idea of all the turnips slowly growing. Choose one instrument, such as a cymbal to play very loudly indeed to show how much bigger one of the turnips has grown.

- Next be sure that everyone knows who they are representing – the man, the wife, boy, the girl, the dog, the cat and the mouse. (Add your own invented characters according to the numbers in your class.)

- The man is the first to play, followed by the big turnip. Next the man and his wife both play together, followed again by the big turnip. Continue like this accumulating more and more instruments into the 'chain' of 'pullers'. Finally when everyone has joined in, there should be a sudden silence followed by a loud clattering from all the instruments representing the chain of 'pullers' falling over as the enormous turnip comes out of the earth. Follow this with a calm, contented section of music, everyone enjoying their turnip feast!

- You can direct the music if you want by indicating to the children using signs who should play and when, also how loudly or quietly, quickly or slowly.

Extension

Appraising and recording your performance

- When you have played your piece through once, talk about how you could improve it. Make sure the children are aware that there is a start, a middle and an ending. The ending is particularly important because it shapes the piece.

- Record your piece when you are happy with it. Of course it won't turn out exactly the same each time you play it. It will fall part way between an improvisation and a composition – i.e. there will be a rough structure to it.

Chapter 5
Sessions 41–50

Focus:
- Feelings in music
- Composition/Choreography/Improvisation
- Meter

Session 41

Concept:
- Feeling sets of four beats

Theme: Feeling happy

Resource: CD track 30

Cheerful Chum

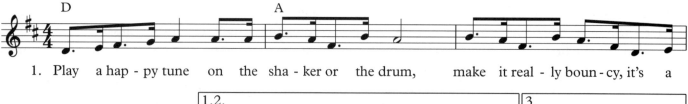

1. Play a hap-py tune on the sha-ker or the drum, make it real-ly boun-cy, it's a

tune for Cheer-ful Chum! Chum!

2. Play a happy tune on the tambourine or drum,
   Make it really bouncy it's a tune for Cheerful Chum!

3. Play a happy tune on the woodblock or the drum,
   Make it really bouncy, it's a tune for Cheerful Chum!

- First learn the song with the help of the CD, track 30.
- Now sit in a circle. Play the CD again, and clap 4 beats each round the circle, in time to the beat of the music, and counting out loud up to 4. (This will take up 17 sets of 4.)

Adding percussion to the song

First in two groups

- Divide the class into two groups and give each group instruments. Play the track again and let them practise taking turns at playing four beats each in time to the music.

Now in six groups

- Next divide the class into six groups and give out the following instruments:

  Group 1: shakers
  Group 2: drums/tambours
  Group 3: tambourines
  Group 4: drums/tambours
  Group 5: woodblocks
  Group 6: drums/tambours

- Groups one and two should alternate playing 4 beats each during verse 1, groups three and four, during verse 2 and groups five and six, during verse 3.

Six groups accompanying 'Cheerful Chum'

Doing actions to the beat
- This is a happy song. Play the CD (track 30) again and all skip round the room to verse 1. Ask the children to choose a different action for verse 2, and to listen carefully to notice when verse 3 starts, being ready to change to another different action.

Extension

Structuring the actions to fit the song
- Can you work out a sequence of 6 different actions with the children? Repeat each action 4 times. Try the sequence through 3 times with the CD, track 30. With this structure, the actions will even fill the short joining bit between verses. At the very end of the song, you will find that there is only enough music to fit in 4 of the actions. For a grand ending, crouch down then jump up, stretching arms up high.

Session 42

Concept:

- Exploring Happy/Sad sounds/Feelings

Theme: Happy and sad

Resource: tape recorder and tape

Talking about feeling happy and sad

- Sit in a circle with a whole range of instruments in the middle. Talk about how we look when we are happy. Try the following expressions and actions: smiling, skipping, dancing, cheering, punching the air, 'hugging' yourself, or less obviously, being very still with 'smiling' eyes. Talk about, and then show, sadness by drooping heads, shoulders and mouths, sitting down heavily, sighing and cupping chin in hands. Now walk round the room in a sad, droopy way, and then skip round the room brightly.

Exploring Happy/Sad sounds

- Now let's consider instruments. It is virtually impossible to say whether a sound heard in isolation is either happy or sad. It is more to do with sounds in context with other sounds – the way the instrument is played, rather than the sound of the instrument itself. So we need to do a bit more exploring. First of all give out the instruments at random. Anyone with a drum should scrape round and round the skin of the drum with their nails, and at the same time, anyone with finger chimes should play them very quietly and slowly. Ask the children if this makes them feel happy or sad. It will probably be perceived as sad. Now ask the woodblocks to play with tambourines. The woodblocks should start first playing at quite a fast pulse, then the tambourines should join in, alternating shaking the bells with tapping the tambourine. This will hopefully be perceived as a happy sound! But it doesn't matter if it isn't! The whole thing is subjective.
- Continue to explore different combinations of sound, sometimes playing quietly, sometimes loudly, sometimes quickly, sometimes slowly. Try with no beat at all.
- Now choose five or six different sound elements from those you have tried out, then decide on the order of these elements to make your piece.
- Try the piece through 2 or 3 times until the children feel as though they are thinking ahead and 'taking charge' of the music. Decide on a title for the piece.
- Record it and listen back.

Extension

Exploring feelings evoked by existing music

- Listen to music of your choice. Does it make you feel happy or sad, or something else? Scared? Angry? Peaceful? Mischievous?

Session 43

Concept:
▪ Feelings in music

Theme: Seasons; happy and sad

Resource: CD tracks 31 and 28

Charlie Chicken and Friends

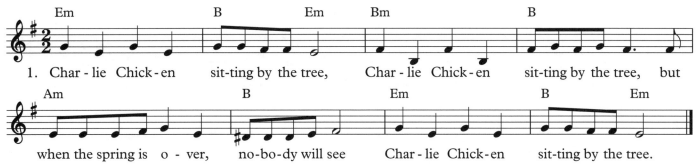

2. Chelsea Chaffinch singing in the tree,
   Chelsea Chaffinch singing in the tree,
   When the summer's over, nobody will see
   Chelsea Chaffinch singing in the tree.

3. Sophie Spider climbing up the tree . . .
   When the autumn's over . . .

4. Rachel Robin flying to the tree . . .
   But when the winter's over . . .

Comparing this new song with a previous one
- Look back to session 39. Play the CD, track 28 to remind the children of the song *Back Another Day.*
- Now play *Charlie Chicken and Friends* on track 31.
- Discuss the differences and similarities of the two songs. The sentiments and the characters are the same in both. But this second song is much sadder sounding. *Back Another Day* has a bright skipping tune, whereas *Charlie Chicken and Friends* is much slower and smoother.

Adding percussion to the song
- Accompany the song with a slow beat as follows:

  <u>Char</u> - lie <u>Chick</u> - en <u>sit</u> - ting by the <u>tree</u>...

  Try finger chimes for verse 1, very quiet cymbals for verse 2, shakers for verse 3 and everyone playing very quietly indeed for verse 4.

A vocal accompaniment
- All whisper the words 'Charlie Chicken' throughout verse 1, the words, 'Chelsea Chaffinch' throughout verse 2, and so on...
- Try both the percussion and the vocal accompaniments at the same time.

Feel the Happy/Sad contrast
- Sing *Back Another Day* again.

Extension

Doubling the speed of the vocal accompaniment
- Play the CD (track 31) and all whisper 'Charlie Chicken' twice as fast as before throughout verse 1, and continue in the same way whispering the relevant words at this faster speed throughout the other three verses.

Session 44

Concept:
- Speed/Co-ordination; Happy/Sad

Theme: Celebration; a street party

Resource: CD track 32

Street Party

1. Let's have a par - ty, let's have a par - ty, let's have a par - ty, a par - ty in the street.

CHORUS: Clap, clap, roll your hands, clap, clap, roll your hands, clap, clap, roll your hands and stamp your feet.

2. Let's find a partner,
   Let's find a partner,
   Let's find a partner,
   A partner in the street.
   CHORUS

3. Let's make a foursome . . .
   CHORUS

4. Let's make a circle . . .
   CHORUS

- This is a great song for singing quickly. During verse 1 do gallops from side to side and finish in a space ready to do the 'Clap clap, roll your hands' section. During verse 2 find someone near to you and hold both their hands and gallop round together, then stop and stand side by side for the 'Clap clap, roll your hands' section. Continue like this to the end of the song.

A percussion accompaniment
- Divide the class into four groups and give each group like sounding instruments as usual. Group one should accompany verse 1 playing the most natural beat, which is fairly fast. All four groups then accompany at this same speed for the chorus, then group two should accompany the second verse and so on.

A Happy/Sad contrast
- Sing *Charlie Chicken and Friends* (with one or both accompaniment options, if you want) to feel the happy/sad contrast.

Extension

- Devise another performance of *Street Party* using instruments, actions and singing. You might even want to add a clapped ostinato.

Session 45

Concept:
- Creating music for movement

Theme: Kaleidoscopes

Resource: A kaleidoscope or pictures of kaleidoscope effects, tape recorder and blank tape

Creating a kaleidoscope piece of music
- First look at kaleidoscope effects and talk about how the patterns and colours merge into each other.

Practise making smooth sounds
- We spent some time exploring sounds in session 42. What we want here is to create a 'wash' of sound, like painting a canvas with big soft swirls in pastel colours. First decide which instruments you want to use then practise playing as smoothly as possible with no sudden loud notes.

Combining the sounds to make a piece
- To impose some structure on that, you be the conductor indicating to the children when they should play/stop playing. Every child should take responsibility by keeping their eyes on you all the time. When it is their turn, they can play to a slow beat or fast beat, or just haphazard notes with no pattern, as long as it is quiet and smooth sounding. Gentle scrapes and continuous sounds are better than sudden short sounds.
- Try to create a dovetailing effect, where the various sounds overlap.

Record your piece
- When you have had a bit of time to practise, try taping your piece. Make sure the ending is distinctive, so that when you move to it later, you will be able to make a lovely ending.

Improvise kaleidoscope movement
- Focus on circles. Find a space of your own and see how many different kinds of circles you can make with your body. Always move slowly and smoothly. Here are some examples: draw a cartwheel in the air with a big slow movement, spin slowly round with arms out at sides (for a short time only!), turn your wrists, your shoulders, your heads – even your ankles, roll your hands over and over each other, do a stirring action at a medium or low level.
- Blend your movements smoothly into each other so that there is no sense of there being separate elements. Bear in mind that you don't have to always face the same way and you can change your level whenever you want.

Circular movements (Kaleidoscope)

Move to your kaleidoscope piece of music

• Play your recorded music and try out the movements.

Extension

• Impose some structure on to these improvised movements. Decide on a beginning, a middle and an ending, so that it becomes more of a choreography than an improvisation. One effective way to do this is to blend in and out of class shapes such as a circle, two lines, pairs/groups, while still doing the individual shapes/movements.

Session 46

Concept:
- Improvising music with more elements

Theme: Celebration; fireworks

Resource: Tape recorder and blank tape

A fireworks dance
- This time let's work the other way round. Start with the movement, using the idea of fireworks as the basis of your piece.
- For Catherine wheels draw on the circle ideas from the last session, but this time they should be done much more quickly. For Roman Candles spring up straight from a crouched position then sink down again. For rockets, jump as high as you can into the air, then use hands and feet to show lots of small explosions. For sparklers, the whole body shakes, while hands shoot out at different levels. Or you can pretend to be holding the sparkler, rather than actually being a sparkler, by twisting, turning and making swirls and scrolls high and low, behind you, in front of you, or reaching out to the side.

The fireworks music
- Start by recalling the wash of sound you created in the last session, Now, remembering the sudden bursts of movement for the different types of firework, decide which sounds would most effectively convey these fireworks.
- Now conduct the piece. Everyone plays the 'wash' of sound until you signal a child or a group of children to make a burst of sound to represent one of the fireworks. Shape your piece like this.

Record your piece
- Play the tape back and see if it feels right to move to.

Extension

- As in the last session, work your fireworks movement ideas into a choreographed dance.

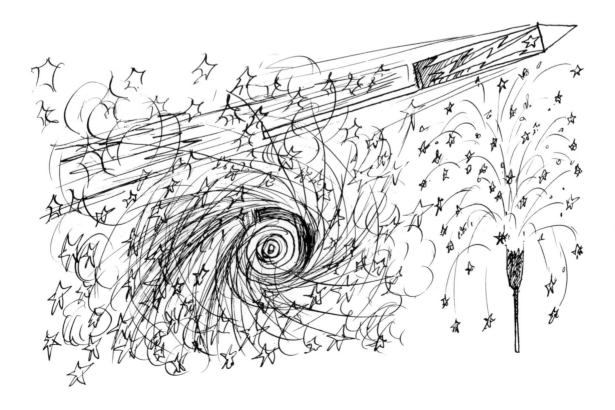

Session 47

Concept:
- Complicated ostinato
- Developing movement vocabulary

Theme: Celebration; Divali

Resource: CD track 1; a few pre-chosen CDs that have extracts of music that you think might be suitable for the Divali candlestick dance (see below)

Celebration

Back to Musical Parade*!*

- If you haven't sung the song *Musical Parade* (from Session 3) for a while, remind yourself of how it goes (with the help of the CD, track 1 if necessary.)

Musical Parade
Tune: This Old Man

Hey, hey, hey!   What a day!   All the child-ren on dis-play, It's a

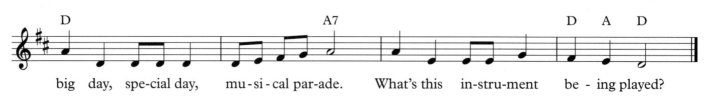

big day, spe-cial day,   mu-si-cal par-ade.   What's this in-stru-ment be-ing played?

Playing three ostinatos
- Divide the class into three groups and give out the instruments – for example, one group with tambourines, one with claves, one with drums. Practise playing the rhythm of the words 'Hey hey hey!' as a repeated ostinato, then practise the rhythm of the words 'big day, special day', similarly as a repeated ostinato, and finally try the rhythm of the words 'musical parade'.
- Now try having a complete run-though with the CD where the groups take turns to accompany one verse with one of the three ostinatos.
- Try it through again, swapping the groups round.

Divali candlestick dance

Divali candlestick dance

- First tell the children about Divali – a festival of light. Show pictures or talk about candelabras or menorahs. Explain/show how these can consist of two, three, five or more candles. The children should sit in a space of their own. If you play one chime on the finger chimes they should stand up tall and straight representing single candles. If you play two chimes they should form pairs, standing tall and straight side by side with a partner. If you play three, they should stand in threes and so on.
- Now see what different *shapes* of candelabra it is possible to make, e.g. three children might be arranged with one standing in the middle and the other two kneeling on either side. So there is a choice of level – sitting, kneeling down, kneeling up or standing, and a choice of shape – a row, a square with one on the middle, or another arrangement.
- Choose some children to be matches and have a signal for those children to run around touching each candle on the head to light it. When a child has been touched on the head, he/she should raise his/her arms up slowly or quickly, either by stretching them out at the sides or with rising 'praying' hands.
- Show the flickering of the candle flames by bending and stretching the elbows.
- Mix up the candle ideas as you want, to make a dance.

Music for your dance

- This time find some suitable music of your choice rather than composing your own. Play the children a few short extracts of music that you think might be suitable for the dance, and see which one they choose. Encourage them to consider the mood and feel of the music, but also talk about the pitch of the music (High/Low) the dynamics of the music (Loud/Quiet) and the speed of the music.
- Try out your movement ideas to your chosen music.

Extension

Musical Parade without the CD

- Divide the class into three groups. For the first sing-through, group one should sing, group two play one of the ostinatos given at the beginning of this session and group three another of those ostinatos. Then swap the groups round for two further sing-throughs.

Session 48

Concept:
- Metre

Theme: Grand, majestic music
Resource: CD tracks 33 and 8

Button Up, Your Majesty!

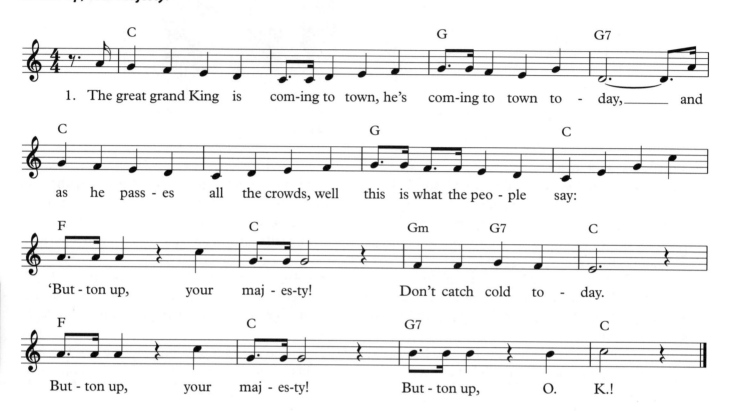

2. Fasten up . . .
3. Buckle up . . .
4. Zipper up . . .
5. Wrap up . . .

- This is a strongly rhythmic song, pursuing the idea of celebration, but with less of an abandoned happy feeling and more of a grand, majestic feel.

To show the metre

- When you have learnt the song, put on the CD, track 33 and march round, keeping exactly to the faster beat for verse 1. Now sit down and see if you can count, in whispers, up to 4 repeatedly throughout verse 2. We say that the song has a 4-time metre, or that it is in 4-time, and this is what you are trying to feel.
- For verse 3, keep counting but clap only on the first of each group of 4 beats.
- For verse 4, half the children should continue to clap on the first beat only and the others should clap on every beat. Try to keep the counting inside your heads.

Showing the 4-time metre with instruments

- Divide the class into two groups. Give instruments to all the children – preferably in two blocks of sound as usual. For verse one, one group should play on the first beat of each set of 4, and the other group should play on every beat. Swap parts for verse 2, then swap back for verse 3 and so on.
- Play the CD track 8 – *The Shape Song*. Is this song in 4-time? Try counting up to 4 repeatedly in whispers as the CD plays. It doesn't work! See if the children can work out for themselves that the song is in 3-time. (i.e. it has a 3-time metre.)

Extension

Button Up, Your Majesty! – a performance

- On the CD, track 33, there is a very short section of accompaniment bridging the verse each time. You might like to try the whole song in four groups:

Group 1: singing
Group 2: marching
Group 3: playing the first beat of each 4
Group 4: playing on all 4 beats

Use the short 'bridging' section to swap groups between verses, so everyone gets a go at all four activities. For the fifth verse, repeat the format for verse 1.

Session 49

Concept:
- Feeling 4-time metre

Theme: Grumpy, happy

Resource: CD tracks 34 and 35

Grumpy and Happy

- First sing the song through. This is another strongly rhythmic song. This time the emotion is grumpiness, as opposed to sadness.

Clap to show the metre
- Sit down and practise clapping on the first of every set of 4 beats, as we did in the previous song.

Actions to feel the metre
- Stand in a space of your own and fold your arms. Simply lift your folded arms up and drop them back very quickly. This action will come on the words 'I', 'limp', 'who', and 'lump'.
- Next stamp with alternate feet (4 times) This takes up the rest of the grumpy part of the song.
- For the happy part, do an action on *every* beat. Work out two different actions, e.g. clapping, patting the floor. Do a set of 4 of the first idea and a set of 4 of the second, then repeat all that 3 more times, which will take you to the end of the song.

Transferring the action ideas to percussion
- Simply divide the class into two groups with different sounding instruments for each group, as usual. One group should play their instruments on exactly the same beats as they did their actions – so play only on the first beat of each group of 4 for the first half of the song, then play on all beats for the second half. The second group should do the opposite – so play on every beat during the first half of the song, and on every first of 4 beats during the second half.

Extension

- Listen to the two short treble recorder pieces on the CD track 35. Talk about the pieces, how do they make you feel?

Session 50

Concept:
- Emotions in music

Theme: Feelings

Resource: The tape of the kaleidoscope music you recorded in session 45 (optional)

Talk about being happy, sad, cross, scared

- Look back to session 42. We talked about how our faces and bodies look when we are happy and when we are sad. Go over those ideas. Then talk about how we look when we are angry or grumpy. Stamp your feet, shake your fists, scowl, fold your arms, put your hands on your hips, wag a finger. What about when we are scared? Tense your bodies, especially shoulders, turn the head suddenly as though startled by a sound, open eyes wide, cover eyes, make a small/thin shape as though hiding.

- Now decide on one pose and expression for each of those four emotions and remember it for the next activity.

Scared expression

Cross expression

An activity with those four emotions

- Ask the children to walk round the room. They might be pretending to rush to school (or adults to work), they might be dawdling or strolling, taking the dog for a walk or doing the shopping. Use the tape of the kaleidoscope music you recorded in session 45, as a background to this if you want. When you pause the tape and play, say, a loud beat on the drum, the children should stop walking and adopt the chosen pose/expression of anger. After a few seconds clap your hands, or put the tape back on, to indicate that they must set off walking again. Continue like this, for example, playing the tambourine as the signal to stop walking and show happiness, the triangle or finger chimes as the signal for sadness and the guiro (scraper) or the shaker as the signal for fear. Change the order of the instruments to encourage the children to really listen.

Music for those four emotions

- In the same way that you explored happy and sad sounds in session 42, explore scary and angry sounds now. The following suggestions might provide starting points:

  Fear: beat the drum at a slow tempo, playing the following rhythm: slow quick quick slow quick quick etc. Emphasise the slow beat each time. Play the cymbal with a soft beater very gently and quite quickly. Gradually play more and more loudly, finishing with a loud clang.

  Anger: Play sudden fast loud outbursts of sound on clattering wooden instruments and/or start gently and slowly and build up to this kind of sound. When combined with a few cymbal crashes this is even more effective.

- Home made instruments/sounds are very useful here. Make up a piece that might concentrate on only one or two of the emotions discussed or might be a sound collage of many different overlapping emotions.

Extension

- Try the activity above where the children walked round and on a given signal adopted the expression of one of the four emotions, only ask one of the children to give the signal each time.

Chapter 6
Sessions 51–60

Focus:
- Extension/Consolidation
- Smooth/Jumpy

Session 51

Concept:
- A new metre – 2-time
- Smooth/Jumpy

Theme: Smooth and jumpy

Resource: CD tracks 36 and 37

You Can Jump with Me

2. I am a frog and I'm jumping along . . .   3. I am a kangaroo jumping along . . .

- Sing the song through with the CD track 36.
- Now listen again carefully, without singing. Can the children work out what is the metre of the song? Try counting in whispers up to 2.

Sing and play percussion to feel the 2-time metre
- Divide the class into three groups:

  Group 1: singers
  Group 2: play instruments on the first of each set of 2 beats
  Group 3: play quietly on all beats

- Pause the CD between verses so the groups can swap round.

91

Jump like a grasshopper

- In spaces of their own, ask the children to jump round like grasshoppers, making sure they only jump on the first of every 2 beats, keeping precisely in time with the music. Half the class should show the other half. Ask those children watching if they noticed anyone doing it particularly accurately.

Listening to a piece of music with smooth and bouncy elements

- Listen to track 37 on the CD. Tell the children beforehand that you are going to ask them about the music afterwards. Was it bouncy or smooth or both? How many changes can they spot?

Extension

You Can Jump with Me – working in a tight rhythmic framework

- Divide the class into three groups:

  Group 1: singers
  Group 2: jumpers
  Group 3: players

- Decide whether the playing group will be playing all the beats or just the first of every two. Then try the song through, swapping the groups for every verse. Don't pause the CD between verses. See if the children can get in place for each following verse, during the very short musical 'bridge' between verses.

Session 52

Concept:
- Working on rhythmic and pitch precision

Theme: Grasshoppers, frogs and kangaroos

Resource: CD track 36

A different performance of *You Can Jump with Me*

- Divide the class into three groups: grasshoppers, frogs and kangaroos. Every child in the kangaroo group has a partner in the grasshopper group. The kangaroos are fantastic musicians who sit together with a different type of percussion instrument each. The frogs are fabulous singers who sit together and sing. The grasshoppers stand in a space of their own and wait for their turn to jump round the room.

- Choose a grasshopper to start jumping. Try verse 1 of the song without the CD. While the chosen grasshopper jumps along in time to the beat the frogs all sing. This first grasshopper's partner (a kangaroo) should play his or her instrument in time to the beat to accompany his partner's jumping. Whoever is standing closest to the grasshopper on the words 'You can jump with me' takes over the jumping next, while the first grasshopper sits down. This second grasshopper's kangaroo partner now takes over playing the beat, while the frogs sing verse 1 again. Continue like this until all the grasshoppers have had a jump, and therefore all the kangaroos have had a chance to play their instrument solo. This activity therefore only uses repetitions of verse 1.

- Swap the groups around so everyone gets to do all three activities. Encourage precision of jumping in the grasshopper.

Clapping alternate beats

- Ask the children to sit in two rows facing each other. Play track 36. The two rows should take turns to clap just 1 beat each in time with the song. Keeping precisely in time is tricky when you are only clapping 1 beat at a time.

Playing alternate beats

- Now ask the children to get into pairs. They should face their partner and each have a different sounding instrument from their partner. Decide which person in each pair should be the first to play and which the second. With track 36 play alternate beats as in the previous activity. If there is any pair doing it particularly well ask them to show the others.

Three groups

93

- Consider the distance that a grasshopper, a frog and a kangaroo can jump. Think of this distance as a distance between two notes of different pitches. Play the lowest C on the xylophone as the starting note for all three. The second note for the flea should be the F 3 notes higher. The second note for the frog should be the C 8 notes higher, and for the kangaroo, play the very top note of the xylophone.
- Once the children have heard you play each creature's two-note 'jump' several times, hide the xylophone and play one of the three types of jump and see if the children can work out which it is.

Session 53

Concept:
- Smooth/Jumpy
- 3-time metre

Theme: Worms

Resource: CD tracks 38 and 37. A CD of *The Carnival of the Animals* by Saint-Saëns

I Am a Worm

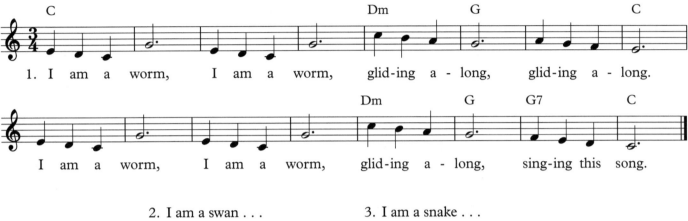

2. I am a swan . . .   3. I am a snake . . .
   Sailing along . . .   Sliding along . . .

- First learn the song with the CD track 38.
- Ask the children what the difference is between this and *You Can Jump with Me*. You are looking for the answer that this is smooth and *You Can Jump with Me* is much bouncier!

What is the metre?

- Now play *I Am a Worm* (track 38) again, and see if the children can work out whether the song is in 2-time, 3-time or 4-time.
- Try counting in whispers up to 3, repeatedly.
- Play the song again and see if the children can co-ordinate 1 knee pat followed by 2 claps throughout. (We first tried this in Session 9. The children's ability to co-ordinate the actions now will be a good indicator of their improvement!)

Listening to musical contrasts in well known music

- The music *The Carnival of the Animals* by Saint-Saëns consists of many short pieces depicting different animals and birds. There are plenty of examples of Loud/Quiet, High/Low, Smooth/Bouncy, Fast/Slow in the music. A particularly good example of a piece in 3-time is 'The Elephant'.
- Also listen to 'The Swan', which is a beautifully smooth piece for the cello, and lends itself well to improvised smooth movement.
- 'The Kangaroo' is a very short bouncy piece. The beats are uneven so it is not a good piece for movement.
- Listen to track 37 again, trying to notice more about the music, such as the dynamics (Loud/Quiet), the gradation of tone (getting louder/quieter), the varying speeds of the music, the changing metre of the music, and the mood of the music.

Extension

- Play track 38 again. Show the children how you can accompany the song with your xylophone; alternating a high C and a low one, playing only on the first of every 3 beats each time.
- Now ask one of the children to play the high C each time, and you play the low one. Finally see if two children can manage to maintain the playing of these alternate beats on the two Cs.

Session 54

Concept:
- three different beats at the same time

Theme: Shopping

Resource: CD track 39

Shopping in the High Street

1. I'd— like to buy some tooth-paste please, I'd— like to buy some tooth-paste please, I'd—

like to buy some tooth-paste please, now tell me what's this shop?

SHOUT: Chemist!

2. I'd like to buy a book of stamps . . . (Post Office)
3. I'd like to buy a loaf of bread . . . (Baker's)
4. I'd like to buy a joint of ham . . . (Butchers')
5. I'd like to draw some money out . . . (Bank)
6. I'd like to buy some salmon please . . . (Fishmonger)

- Sing through the song with the CD, track 39, walking in time to the beat, and stopping at different places in the room pretending they are the shops mentioned in the verses of the song. You might like to put up signs for the various shops around the room.

Three different actions at three different speeds
- The children should stand in spaces of their own. Decide on three very simple actions e.g. kneeling and patting knees, standing and 'air' punching, sitting and tapping heads.
- We are going to do the first action – patting knees – at the slowest speed. To practise this, first play the CD (track 39) and count up to 4 repeatedly to the quick beat of the music. Now ask the children to kneel and pat their knees on the first beat only of each set of 4.
- We are going to do the second action – the 'air' punching – at the medium speed. Again with the CD playing, practise counting up to 4, then punch the air only on beats 1 and 3 of each set of 4.
- We are going to do the head taps at the fastest speed. With the CD, practise doing 1 tap on every beat.
- Now allocate one action to each group and see if all three groups can maintain their own speed of action with the song on the CD. Swap actions for every subsequent verse.

Extension

Percussion at three different speeds
- Transfer the above activity to percussion instruments so one group plays on every beat, one on every other beat and one on the first of every 4 beats. At first, try with just a few children playing and the rest listening, to see if they can really hear all 3 beats.

Session 55

Concept:
- Associating characteristics of animals/people with sound/music

Theme: Bumping and bashing!

Resource: CD tracks 40 and 29

Bertie Bash

- First sing the song through with the CD, track 40. There are little diagrams on the song, showing the actions.
- Sitting down, play the CD and all clap whenever there are three repeated words e.g. 'Bash' 'why' etc. You will see that there are 12 groups of such repeated words.
- Divide the class into four groups, each group with percussion instruments. On the repeated word 'Bash' the first group play 3 beats, on the repeated word 'why' the second group play, and so on. Each group will have 3 turns during the whole song.

Making up a piece using three contrasting characters
- Bertie Bash is a dynamic character. Consider the other characters in the songs of this course. Choose any three, e.g. the light and bouncy grasshopper, the loud slow Bertie Bash and the smooth quiet Worm.
- First make up a simple story to act as a springboard for a musical composition based on the three characters. Here is an example:

97

Bertie Bash is going for a walk in the woods. He keeps tripping over branches because he's quite clumsy. A big branch makes him fall flat on his face. Thump! He stays there on the ground until someone comes along to rescue him.

Meanwhile the Grasshopper is hopping along in the woods when he thinks he hears someone calling for help, but it's only a faint far away call. He ignores it at first and keeps hopping along. But the second time he hears it, he decides to go and investigate and springs off to follow the voice.

At the same time the Worm is wriggling and gliding along, when he too hears the cry for help.

When Bertie has been rescued all three characters break into a celebratory dance!

Extension

- Close your eyes and listen to track 29 of the CD again. Did the music of these extracts remind you of any particular characters, real or imaginary?

Session 56

Concept:
- Associating happenings/stories with musical ideas

Theme: Stories in music

Resource: CD track 10. Stories (see the second sub-heading below)

Do You Know the Story?
Tune: What Shall We Do With The Drunken Sailor?

1. I am a wood cut-ter chop-ping trees down, I am a wood cut-ter chop-ping trees down,

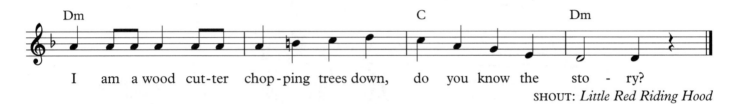

I am a wood cut-ter chop-ping trees down, do you know the sto - ry?

SHOUT: *Little Red Riding Hood*

2. I climbed a beanstalk and found the giant . . . (*Jack and the Beanstalk*)
3. I'm very sad 'cause I'm stuck here cleaning . . . (*Cinderella*)
4. I'm working hard on my house of bricks . . . (*Three Little Pigs*)
5. I'm spinning straw into gold by morning . . . (*Rumplestilskin*)
6. I am a prince cutting down this big hedge . . . (*Sleeping Beauty*)

- First remind yourselves of the song *Do You Know the Story?* (CD track 10 from session 11.)
- Using your own ideas, add percussion.

Making your own sound stories
- The stories mentioned in that song are *Red Riding Hood*, *Jack and the Beanstalk*, *Cinderella*, *Three Little Pigs*, *Rumplestiltskin* and *Sleeping Beauty*. Choose a part of one of these stories which inspires you to make up some music to represent it. Discuss it with the children, talking about which parts of which stories would make particularly good 'sound' stories and why. For example you might like the idea of the beanstalk growing up into the clouds because the xylophone would give the idea of going up, and the clouds could be depicted by soft drum beats. The part of the giant might be played by a very loud different sounding drum and/or a cymbal. This discussion is valuable because the children are making strong associations between people/events and musical sounds.

Extension

- You might like to divide the class into two groups of children and work on two different story lines. Each group could give a concert for the other group, which should generate more discussion about the 'sound' stories.

Session 57

Concept:
- Quick reactions
- Internalisation

Theme: Copying, Olly the parrot

Resource: CD track 41

Please Don't Copy Me

No you can't get cross with me,— I can make you laugh you see,— I can

stand on my head and re-peat what you said, 'cause I'm the cle-ver-est par-rot there could be!

1: Ol - ly!   2: Ol - ly!   1: Don't co-py me!   2: Don't co-py me!   1: Ol - ly!

2: Ol - ly!   1: Please don't co - py   me! 2: Please don't co-py me!   me! 2: O.   K.! No you

- First sing the song with the CD, track 41.

Using percussion to play imitative rhythms

- Divide the class into two groups and give all the children instruments, so we hear two distinctive blocks of sound, as usual. All tap lightly in time with the most natural beat during the first part of the song. For the 'copying' part of the song, the first group should play the exact rhythm of the words of the woman's voice on the CD, and the second group should imitate that rhythm, with the man's voice. Then finish off the song by all tapping lightly together again, for the repeat of the first section of the song.

Internalisation

- Learn that second ('copying') part of the song thoroughly and try singing it without the help of the CD.
- See if the two groups can play the exact rhythm of the words of this 'copying' section, just as before, but without the help of the CD. Count them in by counting to 4 at a steady beat. They should sing the words inside their heads as they play their instruments.

Extension

An internalisation activity – 'Open the door, shut the door'

- Choose a familiar and quite simple song from further back in the course and sing it through to remind yourselves of it.

- Imagine a group of children singing in a room that has a very solid door! When you open the door you can hear them, but when you shut it you can't! Tell the children that when you do a signal as though opening the door, they should start singing the song, and when, after a few seconds, you do a signal as though shutting it, they should immediately stop singing, but carry on inside their heads. Explain that the children in the room are still singing, it's just that they can't be heard. When you then do a signal opening the door again, a few seconds later, the children will be further along in the song. Continue like this, opening and shutting the door at unpredictable times. The skill here is keeping the song going inside your head at exactly the same pace as when it is being sung out loud, so that when the door is opened all the children come in on the same bit!

Session 58

Concept:

- Quick reactions
- Precision
- Imagination
- Confidence
- Thinking ahead
- Working in a tight rhythmic framework

Theme: Action!

Resource: CD track 41 plus other tracks as necessary (see bullet point two)

Please Don't Copy Me

- First sing the song through with two groups playing the percussion accompaniment as in the last session.

Copying the person in the circle

- First decide on a longish song, e.g. *Shopping in the High Street* (track 54), *Lots of Forms of Transport* (track 27) or *We're Going on a Holiday* (track 4) Ask the children to find a space of their own. Put the music on and try out various different actions. *Either* the children can invent their own actions, such as clapping, marching on the spot, strumming a guitar, opening and closing straight arms like a crocodile, doing little jumps on the spot, shaking fingers, tick-tocking heads etc. *Or* you could lead them in this exercise. Try to invent plenty of new and original actions, but make sure they always fit the beat precisely. Children are often tempted to do complicated jumping/jogging actions which are too quick for the beat, and these should be avoided.
- Armed with this vocabulary of actions we are now going to try the activity 'Copying the person in the circle'. The children should stand in a circle with one child in the middle.
- To decide on which child should go in the middle to start off the activity, you could sing *The Birthday Song* (track 7) and when you come to a month in which only one child jumps up and shouts 'That's me!' choose this child to go into the middle.
- When you put the music on, the child in the middle should start doing any action of his/her choice in time to the beat of the music. The other children should immediately join in doing this action. After a few seconds call out the name of another child. This child should then swap places with the one in the middle and immediately set everyone off doing a different action for a few seconds. The children should have an action in mind right from the start so that if they are chosen they are prepared.
- To extend this, don't call out the name of the child. Instead just nod at someone. This means the children must be very alert and always keeping an eye on you as well as doing the actions to see who will be next to go in the middle each time.

Extension

Another copying activity – follow the leader

- This is more complicated than the previous activity because it takes place within a rhythmic framework, so the children have to be continually thinking ahead.
- First think of some ideas of actions that can be done while walking round following a leader. These will have to involve parts of the body other than legs and feet (which will be required for walking!) The other limitation is that the actions should all be able to be described rhythmically during the course of a poem that you will all be chanting as you snake round the room following the leader. Have a look at this to give you the idea:

> Everybody follow Carly
> Everybody follow Carly
> Everybody follow Carly
> Listen to what she says

Carly then calls out the instruction – e.g. 'Play the drums!'

Continue chanting immediately while still following Carly and pretending to play the drums:

Play the drums and follow Carly,
Play the drums and follow Carly
Play the drums and follow Carly
Now it's someone else.

At this point Carly zips to the back of the line, leaving someone else at the front. Continue chanting, e.g:

Everybody follow Christopher
Everybody follow Christopher
Everybody follow Christopher
Listen to what he says
'Lift your shoulders!'
Lift your shoulders and follow Christopher
Lift your shoulders and follow Christopher
Lift your shoulders and follow Christopher
Now it's someone else.

Christopher goes to the back of the line etc.

From the above illustration you will see that there are all sorts of possibilities of different actions that can be done, but it's an idea to try them out beforehand to check that they work as actions, and to establish how to describe them within the context of the chant. It wouldn't work well, for example, if Christopher were to shout out 'Pretend to be an astronaut in a space ship!' not only would it be too long an instruction to fit into the rhythm of the chant, but also there wouldn't be an obvious enough rhythmic action that an astronaut would actually do while sitting in his spaceship!

Session 59

Concept:
- Time
- Silence

Theme: Clocks

Resource: CD track 42

Clocks All Over the Place

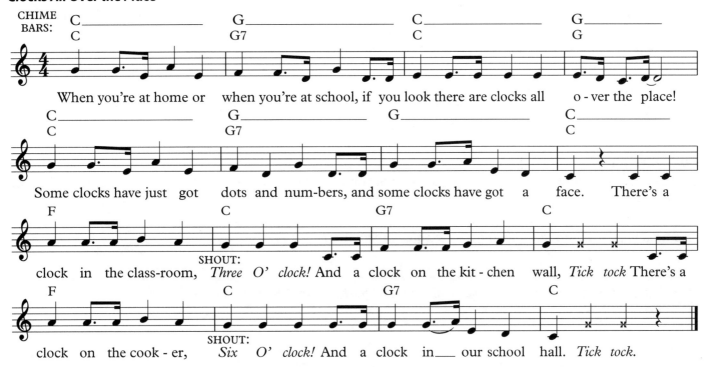

- First learn the song with the CD (track 42) It is sung through 3 times on the CD. The first time you will hear the times 'three o'clock' and 'six o'clock' shouted out. The second and third times nothing is shouted out. This gives you the opportunity to hold up a clock showing any time you want (but *something* o'clock). The children should call out whatever time you are showing at the relevant moment in the song. As they become more adept at telling the time, you can introduce more complicated times such as ten to four, five past eight and so on.

Percussion accompaniment
- Play the ostinato 'three o'clock' during the first part of the song. During the second part play one set of 3 beats at the end of each little phrase.

How long is a minute?
- Walk round and sit down when you think it's up. It always surprises me how different children have wildly varying ideas of how long a minute is! Some will no doubt sit down after about 5 seconds, others would walk round all morning if you let them!

Clock ticking in the silence
- Close your eyes and listen to a clock ticking. Now listen for other sounds happening. Silence is rarely silence!

Extension

- Try a performance of *Clocks All Over the Place*, where some children play chime bars/glockenspiel/xylophone during the first half of the song. The notes (letters) they should play are marked in the music.

105

Session 60

Concept:
- Listening
- Remembering

Theme: Who can remember?

Resource: As necessary (see below)

What's this song?

- Pick a song from the course. The children should listen to you singing the first few notes of the song to 'la'. Alternatively play a tiny extract of the song from the relevant CD track. Can the children recognise which song it is? Increase the clues if necessary.

Which is the favourite song?

- See how many songs the children can remember from the course? Let them vote for a favourite one and two runners up. Sing these three songs, with added percussion if you want.

Quick reactions

- Remind the children of the 'signals game' from Session 5. Add a few more signals and play an extension game of this.

And finally, your school theme song, *The Dingleden Train*!

These last two activities are the link between this book and the Key Stage 1 book in the same series.

Musical Parade (to the tune of 'This Old Man')

Words by Ann Bryant

TRACK 1

Hey, hey, hey! What a day! All the child-ren on dis-play, It's a

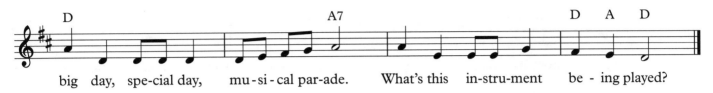

big day, spe-cial day, mu-si-cal par-ade. What's this in-stru-ment be-ing played?

Working Away

Words and Music by Ann Bryant

TRACK 2

1. Sweep-ing, sweep-ing, sweep-ing a-way, sweep-ing a-way, sweep-ing a-way.

Sweep-ing, sweep-ing, sweep-ing a-way, till the work's all done and we can play.

2. Scrubbing, scrubbing . . .
3. Wiping, wiping . . .
4. Baking, baking . . .
5. Ironing, ironing . . .

Songs/Rhymes

How Many Toys? (to the tune of 'Skip To My Lou')

Words by Ann Bryant

Five lit-tle toys are in a row, five lit-tle toys are in a row, five lit-tle toys are in a row, now let us see what hap - pens. Shut, shut, shut your eyes, shut, shut, shut your eyes, here comes a big sur-prise. TEACHER: How ma-ny toys are there now? How ma-ny toys have gone now?

We're Going On A Holiday (to the tune of 'I Saw Three Ships')

Words by Ann Bryant

CHORUS: We're go - ing on a ho - li - day, a ho - li - day, a ho - li - day. We're

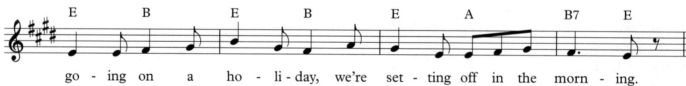

go - ing on a ho - li - day, we're set - ting off in the morn - ing.

1. We're staying in a caravan . . .
   We're setting off in the morning.
   CHORUS

2. We're staying in a big hotel . . .
   CHORUS

3. We're staying on a camping site . . .
   CHORUS

4. We're staying in a seaside house . . .

Songs/
Rhymes

Counting Up The Birthdays

Words and Music by Ann Bryant

TRACK O 5

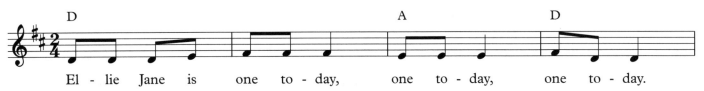

El - lie Jane is one to - day, one to - day, one to - day.

El - lie Jane is one to - day, it's her birth - day.

Make up your own verses depending on your toys/dolls.
e.g. Big brown bear is two today . . .
it's his birthday.

© 2002 International Music Publications Limited

The Birthday Song

Words and Music by Ann Bryant

TRACK O 7

Go - ing to a par - ty, sit - ting in a cir - cle, who's it going to be, let's see.

TEACHER: If you've got a birth-day in the month of *Aug-ust, stand up and shout: 'That's me!'

SHOUT: That's me!

* teacher calls out a different month each time

© 2002 International Music Publications Limited

Songs/Rhymes

The Shape Song (to the tune of 'Poor Jenny Sits A-Weeping')

Words by Ann Bryant

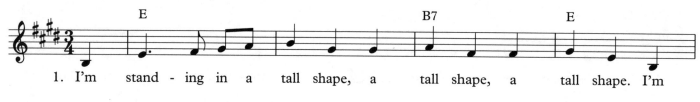

1. I'm stand - ing in a tall shape, a tall shape, a tall shape. I'm

stand - ing in a tall shape, I'm reach - ing up high.

2. I'm standing in a wide space . . .
   I'm stretching out wide.

3. I'm sitting in a small shape . . .
   I'm curling up small.

4. We're standing in a circle . . .
   We're all holding hands.

5. We're crouching in a frog shape . . .
   We're ready to jump.

6. We're sitting in a circle . . .
   Going pat, clap, clap, pat!

Do You Know The Story? (to the tune of 'What Shall We Do With The Drunken Sailor')

Words by Ann Bryant

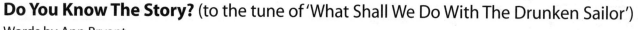

1. I am a wood cut-ter chop-ping trees down, I am a wood cut-ter chop-ping trees down,

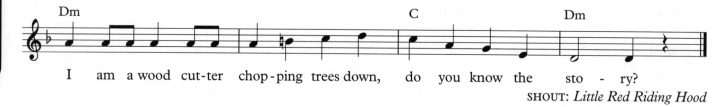

I am a wood cut-ter chop-ping trees down, do you know the sto - ry?

SHOUT: *Little Red Riding Hood*

2. I climbed a beanstalk and found the giant . . . (*Jack and the Beanstalk*)
3. I'm very sad 'cause I'm stuck here cleaning . . . (*Cinderella*)
4. I'm working hard on my house of bricks . . . (*Three Little Pigs*)
5. I'm spinning straw into gold by morning . . . (*Rumplestilskin*)
6. I am a prince cutting down this big hedge . . . (*Sleeping Beauty*)

Songs/Rhymes

The Three Bears' House

Words and Music by Ann Bryant

TRACK 11

1. The three bears' house, it looks like this, it looks like this, it looks like this. The

three bears' house, it looks like this, in the mid - dle of the wood.

2. The smoke from the chimney curls like this . . . In the middle of the wood.
3. The flowers in the garden grow . . .
4. The gate in the garden opens . . .
5. The water fountain sprays . . .
6. The trees in the garden sway . . .
7. The little stream, it runs . . .

© 2002 International Music Publications Limited

Three Little Pigs

Words and Music by Ann Bryant

TRACK 12

1. Three lit - tle pigs, three lit - tle pigs, the first lit - tle pig built a

house of straw. What would you do, what would you do if the

big bad wolf came knock-ing at your door? *Clap clap clap* *clap clap clap.*

2. Three little pigs, three little pigs,
   The second little pig built a house of twigs.
   What would you do, what would you do
   If the big bad wolf came chasing after pigs?

3. Three little pigs, three little pigs,
   The third little pig built a house of bricks.
   What would you do, what would you do
   If the big bad wolf kept getting up to tricks?

© 2002 International Music Publications Limited

Songs/ Rhymes

In The Great, Big Woods

Words and Music by Ann Bryant

1. It's day time in the great big woods but the owl can't get to sleep. _____ The bees buzz, 'buzz buzz buzz' but the owl can't get to sleep.

2. It's day time in the great big woods
   But the owl can't get to sleep.
   The squirrel cracks nuts, 'crack crack crack'
   But the owl can't get to sleep.

3. It's day time in the great big woods
   But the owl can't get to sleep.
   The woodpecker pecks, 'rat-a-tat-tat'
   But the owl can't get to sleep.

4. It's night time in the great big woods
   But the birds can't get to sleep.
   The owl screeches, 'T-wit-t-wit-t-woo!'
   But the birds can't get to sleep.

Animal Noises

Words and Music by Ann Bryant

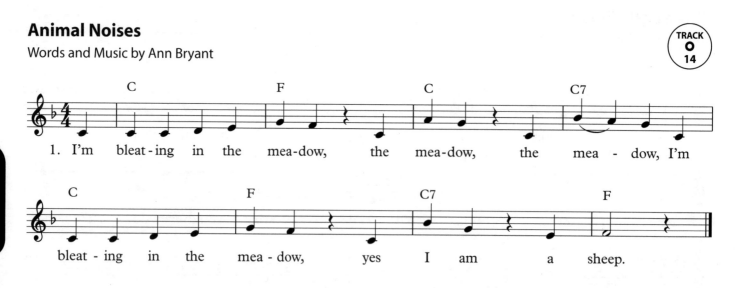

1. I'm bleat-ing in the mea-dow, the mea-dow, the mea - dow, I'm bleat - ing in the mea - dow, yes I am a sheep.

2. I'm purring in the sunshine . . .
   Yes I am a cat.

3. I'm hissing in the jungle . . .
   Yes I am a snake.

4. I'm clucking in the farmyard . . .
   Yes I am a hen.

5. I'm croaking on a lily pad . . .
   Yes I am a frog.

Songs/ Rhymes

What Do You Like To Eat? (to the tune of 'A Sailor Went To Sea')

Words by Ann Bryant

TRACK
15

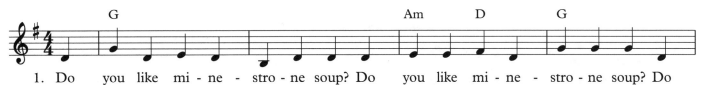

1. Do you like mi - ne - stro - ne soup? Do you like mi - ne - stro - ne soup? Do

you like mi - ne - stro - ne soup? No I like chick - en soup. *Clap clap.*

2. Do you like ham and mushroom pie? . . .
   No I like tuna pie.

3. Do you like peanut butter rolls? . . .
   No I like bacon rolls.

4. Do you like date and walnut cake? . . .
   No I like lemon cake.

5. Do you like choc'late chip ice cream? . . .
   No I like mint ice cream.

6. Do you like lemonade to drink? . . .
   No I like orange squash.

7. Do you like breakfast, lunch or tea? . . .
   I don't like one, I like all three!

Lazy Daisy's Song

Words and Music by Ann Bryant

TRACK
16

1. This is La - zy Dai - sy's song, she does - n't jog, she strolls a - long.

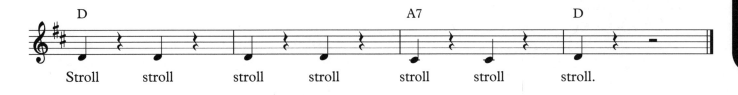

Stroll stroll stroll stroll stroll stroll stroll.

2. This is Lazy Daisy's song,
   She doesn't jog she flops along.
   Flop flop flop flop flop flop flop.

3. This is Lazy Daisy's song,
   She doesn't jog she crawls along.
   Crawl crawl crawl crawl crawl crawl crawl.

Songs/
Rhymes

113

Zippy Zappy

Words and Music by Ann Bryant

TRACK 17

Zip-py Zap-py claps his hands like this *(fast claps)*   Zip-py Zap-py stamps his feet like this *(fast stamps)*

Zip-py Zap-py shakes his head like this *(fast head shakes)*   Zip-py Zap-py makes a shape like this   *(shape)*

The Dingleden Train

Words and Music by Ann Bryant

TRACK 19

Oh the Din-gle-den train goes chug-ging a - long,   chug-ging a - long,   chug-ging a - long, oh the

Din - gle-den train goes   chug-ging a - long,   till the top   meets the   tip.

Songs/
Rhymes

114

Lots Of Forms Of Transport (to the tune of 'Bobby Shaftoe')

Words by Ann Bryant

CHORUS: You may want to tra-vel quick-ly, you may want to tra-vel slow-ly, you may want to

make a jour-ney in a fer-ry boat.
2. in the Eu-ro-star.
3. in a Boe-ing jet.
4. on a mo-tor-bike.

1. Boats go sail-ing on the sea, boats go sail-ing

on the sea, boats go sail-ing on the sea, they're a form of trans-port.

CHORUS:
You may want to travel quickly,
You may want to travel slowly,
You may want to make a journey in the Eurostar.

2. Trains go whizzing on the rails
Trains go whizzing on the rails
Trains go whizzing on the rails
They're a form of transport

CHORUS:
You may want . . .
. . . in a Boeing jet.

3. Planes go soaring in the air . . .

CHORUS:
You may want . . .
. . . on a motor bike.

4. Bikes go roaring on the road . . .

Songs/Rhymes

The Weather Wonder Band

Words and Music by Ann Bryant

TRACK 21

1. When the hail beats down, when the hail beats down, when the
hail beats down in the wea - ther won - der-land, we can beat the drum, we can
beat the drum, we can beat the drum in the wea - ther won - der band.

2. When the wind shakes the trees . . .
We can shake our tambourines . . .

3. When the sun comes out . . .
We can play our bells . . .

4. When the ice goes drip . . .
We can tap our claves . . .

My Minibeast Friends

Words and Music by Ann Bryant

TRACK 22

1. In my gar - den, un - der my tree, you must tip - toe ve - ry care-ful-ly, 'cause
all my friends live un - der that tree, and you don't want to tread on Alf you see, 'cause
Alf is an ant, Alf is an ant, down__ on the ground,
Alf is an ant, Alf is an ant, march - ing all a - round.

2. Will is a woodlouse . . .
Creeping all around.

3. Ben is a beetle . . .
Beetling all around.

4. Sid is a snail . . .
Strolling all around.

Songs/ Rhymes

Felicity Fly (to the tune of 'For He's A Jolly Good Fellow')

Words by Ann Bryant

TRACK 23

Fe - li - ci - ty lives in the tree top, Fe - li - ci - ty lives in the tree top, Fe - li - ci - ty lives in the tree___ top, and I live down be - low.___ Some-times I like to go_____ up high to say hel - lo. Oh, Fe - li - ci - ty lives in the tree top, Fe - li - ci - ty lives in the tree top, Fe - li - ci - ty lives in the tree___ top, and I live down be - low.___

© 2002 International Music Publications Limited

Boogie Bugs

Words and Music by Ann Bryant

TRACK 24

1. Clap your hands for the boo - gie bugs, boo-gy-ing right down on the ground. Clap your hands for the boo - gie bugs, boo-gy-ing a-round and a - round._ Well you boo-gie to the left,_ boo-gie to the right, boo-gy-ing with-out a sound.

2. Swing your hips for the boogie bugs . . .
3. Tick tock heads . . .
4. Jump jump jump . . .
5. Pat your knees . . .
6. Stamp stamp stamp . . .

© 2002 International Music Publications Limited

Songs/Rhymes

117

The Bell Ringer

Words and Music by Ann Bryant

I am a bell ring - er ring - ing my bell, high, low, high, low.

Swing-ing side to side is fun as well. Swing, swing, swing, swing.

© 2002 International Music Publications Limited

Down On The Ground

Words and Music by Ann Bryant

1. Keep - ing to the beat, walk - ing here and there, shake your fin - gers

high up in the air, and then you jump and jump and jump with-out a sound,

roll your shoul - ders round and round and round, and jump and jump and

jump with-out a sound, and then you slow - ly put your fin - gers on the ground.

2. . . . slowly put your hands upon the ground.
3. . . . slowly put your knees upon the ground.
4. . . . slowly put your bottom on the ground.
5. . . . slowly put yourself upon the ground.

© 2002 International Music Publications Limited

Songs/Rhymes

Back Another Day

Words and Music by Ann Bryant

TRACK 28

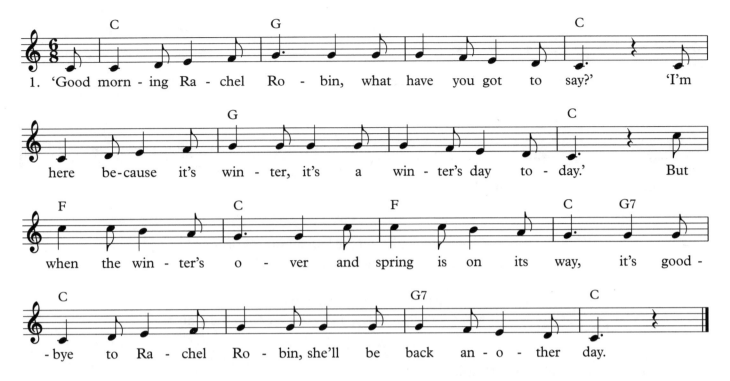

1. 'Good morn - ing Ra - chel Ro - bin, what have you got to say?' 'I'm
here be-cause it's win - ter, it's a win - ter's day to - day.' But
when the win - ter's o - ver and spring is on its way, it's good -
- bye to Ra - chel Ro - bin, she'll be back an - o - ther day.

2. 'Good morning Charlie Chicken, what have you got to say?'
   'I'm here because it's springtime, it's a springtime day today.'
   But when the spring is over and summer's on its way,
   It's goodbye to Charlie Chicken, he'll be back another day.

3. 'Good morning, Chelsea Chaffinch, what have you got to say?'
   'I'm here because it's summer, it's a summer's day today.'
   But when the summer's over and winter's on its way,
   It's goodbye to Chelsea Chaffinch, she'll be back another day.

4. 'Good morning, Sophie Spider, what have you got to say?'
   'I'm here because it's autumn, it's an autumn day today.'
   But when the autumn's over and winter's on its way,
   It's goodbye to Sophie Spider, she'll be back another day.

Songs/Rhymes

Cheerful Chum

Words and Music by Ann Bryant

TRACK
30

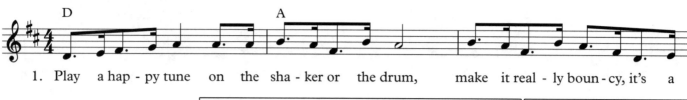

1. Play a hap - py tune on the sha - ker or the drum, make it real - ly boun - cy, it's a

tune for Cheer - ful Chum!   Chum!

2. Play a happy tune on the tambourine or drum,
   Make it really bouncy it's a tune for Cheerful Chum!

3. Play a happy tune on the woodblock or the drum,
   Make it really bouncy, it's a tune for Cheerful Chum!

Charlie Chicken and Friends

Words and Music by Ann Bryant

TRACK
31

1. Char - lie Chick - en sit - ting by the tree, Char - lie Chick - en sit - ting by the tree, but

when the spring is o - ver, no - bo - dy will see Char - lie Chick - en sit - ting by the tree.

2. Chelsea Chaffinch singing in the tree,
   Chelsea Chaffinch singing in the tree,
   When the summer's over, nobody will see
   Chelsea Chaffinch singing in the tree.

3. Sophie Spider climbing up the tree . . .
   When the autumn's over . . .

4. Rachel Robin flying to the tree . . .
   But when the winter's over . . .

Songs/
Rhymes

Street Party

Words and Music by Ann Bryant

1. Let's have a par - ty, let's have a par - ty, let's have a par - ty, a par - ty in the street.

CHORUS: Clap, clap, roll your hands, clap, clap, roll your hands, clap, clap, roll your hands and stamp your feet.

2. Let's find a partner,
   Let's find a partner,
   Let's find a partner,
   A partner in the street.
   CHORUS

3. Let's make a foursome . . .
   CHORUS

4. Let's make a circle . . .
   CHORUS

Button Up, Your Majesty!

Words and Music by Ann Bryant

1. The great grand King is com-ing to town, he's com-ing to town to - day, _____ and as he pass - es all the crowds, well this is what the peo - ple say:

'But - ton up, your maj - es - ty! Don't catch cold to - day.

But - ton up, your maj - es - ty! But - ton up, O. K.!

2. Fasten up . . .
3. Buckle up . . .
4. Zipper up . . .
5. Wrap up . . .

Songs/
Rhymes

121

Grumpy and Happy

Words and Music by Ann Bryant

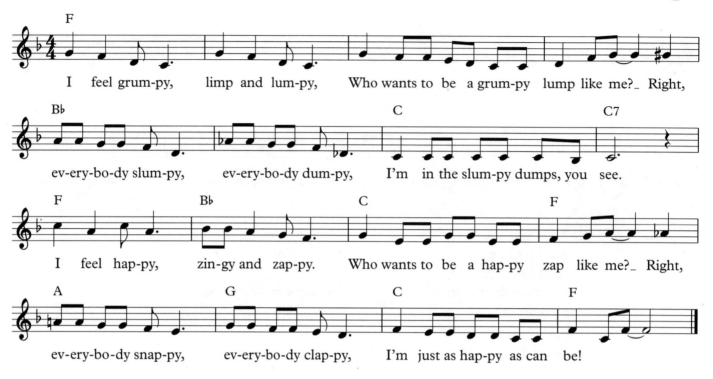

I feel grum-py, limp and lum-py, Who wants to be a grum-py lump like me?_ Right,
ev-ery-bo-dy slum-py, ev-ery-bo-dy dum-py, I'm in the slum-py dumps, you see.

I feel hap-py, zin-gy and zap-py. Who wants to be a hap-py zap like me?_ Right,
ev-ery-bo-dy snap-py, ev-ery-bo-dy clap-py, I'm just as hap-py as can be!

You Can Jump With Me

Words and Music by Ann Bryant

1. I am a grass-hop-per jump-ing a-long, Jump-ing a-long as high as can be.
I am a grass-hop-per jump-ing a-long, you can jump with me.____

2. I am a frog and I'm jumping along . . .   3. I am a kangaroo jumping along . . .

Songs/
Rhymes

I Am A Worm

Words and Music by Ann Bryant

TRACK
38

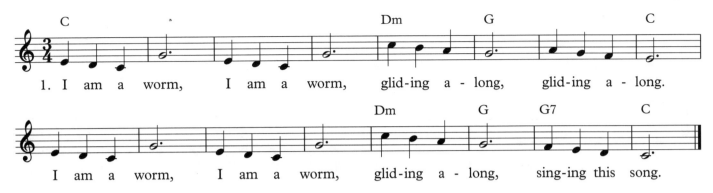

1. I am a worm, I am a worm, glid-ing a - long, glid-ing a - long.
I am a worm, I am a worm, glid-ing a - long, sing-ing this song.

2. I am a swan . . .
   Sailing along . . .

3. I am a snake . . .
   Sliding along . . .

Shopping In The High Street

Words and Music by Ann Bryant

TRACK
39

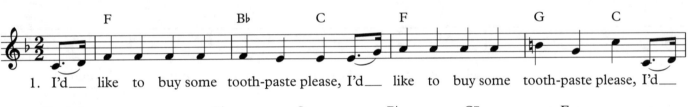

1. I'd__ like to buy some tooth-paste please, I'd__ like to buy some tooth-paste please, I'd__

like to buy some tooth-paste please, now tell me what's this shop?

SHOUT: Chemist!

2. I'd like to buy a book of stamps . . . (Post Office)
3. I'd like to buy a loaf of bread . . . (Baker's)
4. I'd like to buy a joint of ham . . . (Butchers')
5. I'd like to draw some money out . . . (Bank)
6. I'd like to buy some salmon please . . . (Fishmonger)

Songs/
Rhymes

Bertie Bash

Words and Music by Ann Bryant

My name is Ber-tie Bash Bash Bash, I bet you can see why why why! You see I had a

crash crash crash, be-cause I tried to fly fly fly! There's a ban-dage on my

head head head, there's a ban-dage on my nose nose nose, there's a ban-dage on me

knees knees knees, there's a ban-dage on my toes toes toes, there's a ban-dage on my

arms arms arms there's a ban-dage on my tum tum tum. But the fun-ni-est of

all all all is the ban-dage on my thumb thumb thumb!

Songs/
Rhymes

Please Don't Copy Me

Words and Music by Ann Bryant

No you can't get cross with me,— I can make you laugh you see,— I can

stand on my head and re-peat what you said, 'cause I'm the cle-ver-est par-rot there could be!

1: Ol - ly!   2: Ol - ly!   1: Don't co-py me!   2: Don't co-py me!   1: Ol - ly!

2: Ol - ly!   1: Please don't co - py me! 2: Please don't co-py me!   me! 2: O. K.! No you

Clocks All Over The Place

Words and Music by Ann Bryant

When you're at home or when you're at school, if you look there are clocks all o - ver the place!

Some clocks have just got dots and num-bers, and some clocks have got a face. There's a

clock in the class-room, *Three O' clock!* And a clock on the kit - chen wall, *Tick tock* There's a

SHOUT:

clock on the cook - er, *Six O' clock!* And a clock in___ our school hall. *Tick tock.*

SHOUT:

Songs/Rhymes

Ho ho! Here He Comes!

Words and Music by Ann Bryant

TRACK
43

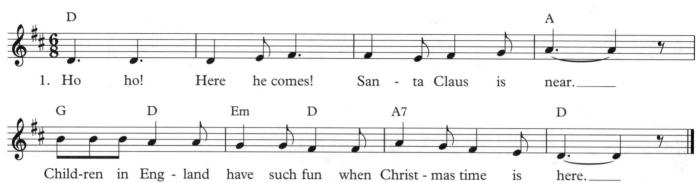

1. Ho ho! Here he comes! San - ta Claus is near.____

Child-ren in Eng - land have such fun when Christ - mas time is here.____

2. Ho ho! Here he comes!
   Sinter Klaus is near
   Children in Holland have such fun
   When Christmas time is here.

3. Ho ho! Here he comes!
   Pere Noel is near.
   Children in France have such fun
   When Christmas time is here.

4. Ho ho! Here he comes!
   Weihnachtsmann is near,
   Children in Germany have such fun
   When Christmas time is here.

The Christmas Train

Words and Music by Ann Bryant

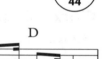
TRACK
44

1. Come and ride on the Christ-mas train, we're going to see the ba - by, we're going to see the ba - by.

Come and ride on the Christ-mas train, we're going to see the ba - by King of Kings.

2. Come and ride on the Christmas train,
   We're going to see the angels, we're going to see the angels,
   Come and ride on the Christmas train,
   We're going to see the angels in the sky.

3. We're going to see the shepherds on the hill.
4. We're going to see the wisemen with their gifts.
5. We're going to see the stable and the star.
6. We're going to see the baby King of Kings.

Whatever Can It Be?

Tapping on my present	*Tap imaginary present*
Whatever could it be?	
Rattling my present	*Rattle present*
Whatever could it be?	
Snipping the ribbons	*Snip ribbons*
Whatever could it be?	
The bounciest ball	*Pretend to bounce a ball*
To bounce in the air?	
A long woolly scarf	*Wrap scarf round neck*
For me to wear?	
Rings for my fingers?	*Wiggle fingers*
Brushes for my heair?	*Brush hair*
A big bright book?	*Open out praying hands*
A cuddly brown bear?	*Cuddle a bear*
Open it up	*Open parcel*
And what do we see	
My own blue camera	*Take a photograph*
Just for me!	

Tidy up for Christmas

I want this house tidied up for Christmas	*Wag finger*
So everybody help and we'll soon get it done	*Wag finger at everyone*
I'll wash the dishes	*Wash dishes*
You dry the dishes	*Wipe dishes*
I'm not drying dishes, that's no fun!	*Hands on hips in protest*
I want this house tidied up for Christmas	*Wag finger*
So everybody help and we'll soon get it done	*Wag finger a everyone*
I'll sweep the floor	*Sweep floor*
You scrub the floor	*Scrub floor*
I'm not scrubbing floors, that's no fun!	*Hands on hips*
I want this house tidied up for Christmas	*Wag finger*
So everybody help and we'll soon get it done	*Wag finger at everyone*
I'll do the vacuuming	*Vacuum carpet*
You do the dusting	*Dust furniture*
I'm not dusting, that's no fun!	*Hands on hips*
I want this house tidied up for Christmas	*Wag finger*
So everybody help and we'll soon get it done	*Wag finger at everyone*
I'll make the cake	*Stir cake mixture*
You ice the cake	*Ice the cake*
I'll *eat* the cake, that's great fun!	*Hold piece of cake nearer and nearer mouth and take bite after saying last word of rhyme*

Index of Themes

Index of Songs/Rhymes

CD Track Listing

Track Title

1. *Musical Parade*
2. *Working Away*
3. *How Many Toys?*
4. *We're Going on a Holiday*
5. *Counting Up The Birthdays*
6. Action music (Session 7)
7. *The Birthday Song*
8. *The Shape Song*
9. *The Wind*
10. *Do You Know The Story?*
11. *The Three Bears' House*
12. *Three Little Pigs*
13. *In The Great Big Woods*
14. *Animal Noises*
15. *What Do You Like To Eat?*
16. *Lazy Daisy's Song*
17. *Zippy Zappy*
18. *Elephants*
19. *The Dingleden Train*
20. *Lots Of Forms Of Transport*
21. *The Weather Wonder Band*
22. *My Minibeast Friends*
23. *Felicity Fly*

24. *Boogie Bugs*
25. *Jing-a-Jing-a-Jungle*
26. *The Bell Ringer*
27. *Down On The Ground*
28. *Back Another Day*
29. Instrumental extracts (Session 39)
30. *Cheerful Chum*
31. *Charlie Chicken and Friends*
32. *Street Party*
33. *Button Up Your Majesty*
34. *Grumpy and Happy*
35. Musical extracts (Session 49)
36. *You Can Jump With Me/Grasshoppers, Frogs and Kangaroos*
37. Music extracts (Session 50)
38. *I Am A Worm*
39. *Shopping in The High Street*
40. *Bertie Bash*
41. *Please Don't Copy Me*
42. *Clocks*
43. *Ho Ho! Here He Comes!*
44. *The Christmas Train*

Appendices

2/04

9311A   ISBN: 1-84328-144-9

"This is, literally, the book that I have been looking for!"
Carol Gray GRSM, LRAM, ARCM, Music Teacher, Bedgebury Junior School

"This is a scheme I would certainly recommend to any Key Stage 1 teacher, specialist or not."
Mel Bussell, Music Coordinator, Southgate Infants School, Derby

"For the non-musicians who have to take on Key Stage 1 music teaching - go for this course. Do not be frightened - it will provide all you need and your children will have a superb musical training.
For the music specialist - this course will give you so many ideas for wonderful interactive games which will so enhance what you offer that I guarantee that your music teaching will never be the same again!"
Helen Mackinnon MA, LRAM, LTCL, Director of Music, Berkhampstead School, Cheltenham